D1499296

Carol Samuel
Managing Director

Communispond, Inc.
160 Sansome Street, 10th Floor
San Francisco, CA 94104 (415) 392-6600
Fax (415) 398-7539

Praise for Socratic Selling

"Socrates is alive and well, and reminds salespeople that selling means talking *with*, not *at*, the customer. With that dialogue approach, a sale is the logical outcome."
James C. Curvey,
President, Fidelity CAPITAL

"Kevin Daley's approach is a breakthrough! The Socratic method enables the salesperson to be open and consistent with the customer at those critical moments when the relationship is tested. Not to be missed are the sections on handling objections, negotiating, and closing 'Socratically'."
Stephen G. Canton,
Vice President, Sales, Allnet

"Since we implemented Socratic selling, the effectiveness of our sales force has substantially improved, resulting in dramatically higher sales in a very sophisticated market."
Thomas J. Lucey,
Senior Managing Director, Putnam Investments

"Kevin Daley is a winner and a great communicator. 'Socratic Selling' will not only help you sell more but make your customers raving fans."
Kenneth H. Blanchard,
Co-author, The One Minute Manager®

"In 'Socratic Selling', Kevin Daley teaches why the truly great sales people listen as well as talk. Socrates had the idea, but Daley shows us how to use it today. The approach works! I know; I tried it."
James W. Kinnear,
Retired CEO, Texaco, Inc.

"The good news is, this book offers no secret techniques or psychological analysis—just a practical way to reach agreement with your customer. Salespeople and customers both win."
Dr. William C. Byham,
CEO, Development Dimensions International

"It's amazing what you can learn when you let your customers do the talking. Kevin Daley's techniques for questioning and listening will help make your sales team more effective."

Peter A. Loquercio,
Director, Access Sales Planning, NYNEX

"Apply these principles and here's Daley describing you: 'You are a valuable resource . . . you are systematic, alert, reliable, worthy of trust. You make the time productive. The customer thinks more clearly when you're there."

Mark Kimble,
Managing Director, Corporate Information,
The Alexander Consulting Group

"Attention, business owners, purchasing agents, training managers: Use this book to decide if the salesperson who calls on you is a potential business partner, or just another somebody making a pitch."

Robert Craig,
Marketing Manager, Omni Business Systems

"The best salespeople are the ones who ask very good questions and really listen to the answers. This book will help salespeople do just that."

Harry H. Gaines,
President, Blessing/White, Inc.

"The results are measurable. Our Socratically trained wholesalers are the most successful."

Donald E. Webber,
Senior Vice President, Eaton Vance Corporation

"All marketing wars take place in the mind of a prospect or customer. 'Socratic Selling' is a powerful, new methodology into that mind."

Jack Trout,
President, Trout & Partners Ltd.

"Sales managers who think their salespeople spend too much time talking and not enough listening should pack 'Socratic Selling' in everybody's flight bag."

David Rupert,
President, Pitney Bowes Management Systems

"'Socratic Selling' shows you a practical way to reach agreement with your customer."

James Molinaro,
Senior Vice President, Sales, Penske Truck Leasing

SOCRATIC SELLING:
How to Ask the Questions that Get the Sale

Kevin Daley

with Emmett Wolfe

IRWIN
Professional Publishing®
Chicago • London • Singapore

Editor-in-chief:	Jeffrey A. Krames
Senior editor:	Cynthia Zigmund
Senior marketing manager:	Tiffany Dykes
Production supervisor:	Lara Feinberg
Assistant manager, desktop services:	Jon Christopher
Project editor:	Rebecca Dodson
Senior Designer:	Heidi J. Baughman
Compositor:	Wm. C. Brown Publishers
Typeface:	11/13 electra
Printer:	Quebecor/Book Press
Cover photo:	Mario Suriani

Library of Congress Cataloging-in-Publication Data

Daley, Kevin, date
    Socratic selling : how to ask the questions that get the sale /
Kevin Daley, with Emmett Wolfe.
        p.   cm.
    Includes index.
    ISBN 0–7863–0455–3
    1. Selling.   I. Wolfe, Emmett.   II. Title.
HF5438.25.D35   1996
658.85—dc20   95–20289

Printed in the United States of America
3 4 5 6 7 8 9 0 QB 2 1 0 9 8 7 6

Contents

Preface

Socratic Selling is a new approach to selling that finds its roots in the successful method of Socrates—talking less and listening more. Every salesperson, no matter what the level of experience, can profit from this new approach. The Socratic approach helps you to join your customer's strengths with your own so that you can work together toward a common goal. Call it "the sale" if you sell. Call it "the buy" if you're the customer. Call it a successful collaboration. The Socratic way can work for you.

I enthusiastically recommend the Socratic approach from experience. The Socratic philosophy and practice of selling has helped thousands of our clients who are salespeople by designation or who bring technical expertise to the sales effort. It's a method that makes sense, can be understood and applied by a busy person, and respects the customer!

We at Communispond practice what we preach. We count on Socratic dialogue to help us best serve our clients, and my greatest satisfaction has been in witnessing "Socratic" become part of the sales culture of so many companies.

The method and rationale of Socratic selling is presented in four parts:

• Part I, "Taking the Socratic Approach," focuses on why the Socratic method is ideal for today's rough-and-tumble sales world. Three chapters give you a realistic view of salespeople, customers, and the dialogue method that enables you to be productive for your company.

• Part II, "Opening the Sale Socratically," examines the crucial beginning of the sales dialogue. Three chapters show you the forces at play when salesperson meets customer, when the salesperson uses the dynamic "Socratic opener," and when salesperson and customer immediately follow up on the Socratic opening.

• Part III, "Advancing the Sale Socratically," develops the expertise that lets the Socratic salesperson guide the dialogue. In the chapters on urgency, feelings, listening, and decision making, you as salesperson experience the sales dialogue as the customer does. These chapters lead, fittingly, to a whole new treatment of the sales proposal as a customer-centered event.

• Part IV, "Closing the Sale Socratically," gives you a unique approach to handling questions, objections, and negotiating with customers. The final chapter gives you a fail-safe way to close that is natural and pressure-free. It effectively uses the momentum gained in the Socratic dialogue.

The Prologue and the Epilogue to the four parts of the book narrate a Socratic sales event that took place in 400 B.C. Bear with me here. You'll just have to believe, without documentation on my part, that Socrates influenced salespeople even during his lifetime! Who is to say such an influence could not have occurred? Athens, 24 centuries ago, was a center of commerce; salespeople were selling; and Socrates was well known to his fellow Athenians.

Faced with the task of acknowledging those who in some way shaped this book, I have to choose between a long or short list. For the reader's sake, the list is short. Because so many of my colleagues have contributed, I would like to step back from the book itself to view the Socratic Selling Skills program upon which the book is based. I'm thankful to the account executives and faculty of Communispond, who, by making the program a success, have made a book worthwhile. In particular, I'm grateful to Carol Samuel for her ideas, energy, and commitment. Without Carol there would be no Socratic Selling Skills program.

I have discussed Socratic selling with hundreds of clients and appreciate their feedback. More recently, some clients shared their thoughts in connection with the writing of this book. In that regard, thanks to James Wood of Penske Truck Leasing; Jeff

Bradshaw and Charles Benz of Monsanto; Carman Read of Monsanto Canada, Inc.; Sarano Kelley of PaineWebber; and Larry McGinnes of JM Family Enterprises, Inc. A dozen salespeople at Ameritech expressed their thoughts on a video cassette. Needless to say, I found it productive and enjoyable viewing.

For their thoughts on the international impact of Socratic selling, thanks to David Charner of The English Resource Center in Caracas, Venezuela; Masumi Muramatsu of Simul International, Inc., in Tokyo for a beautiful rendering of the Socratic questions in Japanese; Dietske Van Kessel of Van Kessel & Partners, Wassenaar, Netherlands; and my colleague Andrew Telford of London, U.K., whose staff has carried Socrates to many European cities. Next stop, Athens.

Kevin Daley

Prologue: 400 B.C.

In 400 B.C., *the time of Socrates, a sales manager and a salesperson are returning to Athens from a sales call in the surrounding hills. The fatigue of the long road back has set in. The sales manager, Crito, pulls his toga tighter around his shoulders. The salesperson, Darius, concentrates on steering the wagon away from the deep ruts.*

Darius can bear the silence no longer. "Well, how'd it go?"

"It didn't go well," *says the sales manager.*

"It went as well as it could. I told them transporting the stone from their quarries to the building site is the costliest part of their business. I told them they are the largest building company in the state and yet broken wheels are killing them—20, 30 of their masons standing around one of their building sites in Athens and no stone to work with. The stone doesn't get there. The stone's in a broken-down wagon up in the hills. You'd think those people would know their own business. They can't run their business without the best wagon wheels. You'd think I wouldn't have to keep explaining what we can do for them."

Crito is looking up at the hillside. "You didn't begin the meeting right," *he says.*

"What do you mean I didn't begin right?" *Darius asks, shaking the reins and jolting the wagon into motion.* "Remember when we shook hands and sat down with the six of them and they invited me to begin? I told them about our company. Then I rolled one of our wagon wheels along the meeting table to grab their attention! Later on, when I struck the metal runner with a rock to show how strong the wheel is, that old guy at the end of the table nearly jumped out of his toga. Nobody sleeps during my sales presentations."

"And you didn't end right," Crito says, now looking down at the road.

"What do you mean I didn't end right? They just weren't ready to buy. They said they'd think it over. Some people can't make up their minds."

Now Crito is looking at the sky. "And between the way you began and the way you ended, the middle part of the meeting didn't go well either."

"How can you say that!" exclaims Darius. "I kept telling them our story. I know it by heart."

"You could double your sales, Darius."

"By the gods, I had a good year! I got the silver mine business at Laurium. I got the pottery fair business."

"There are three mining enterprises at Laurium. You got the business of one. You got the pottery fair business for the spring season. What happened to the summer season? As for the fall pottery fairs, it's almost winter, Darius. Notice how dark it gets."

"I talked to the top people at all the mines at Laurium. I talked to all the organizers of all the pottery fairs in Athens."

"Perhaps that's the trouble, Darius—you talk. Your enthusiasm is an asset that gets in your way. I don't want to dampen your spirits. I recognize your achievements. But you have the energy and the wit to achieve much more."

"Then give me some more tips."

"Darius, it's not about tips. I've taught you what I know about our business. You must learn a more important step—how to connect what you know to what the customer knows."

"What does the customer know?"

"The customer knows the truth. And when the customer reveals the truth, you discover more opportunities to close sales than you at first imagine. But your enthusiasm for telling what you know keeps you from that discovery. You need a teacher."

"Oh, no, not somebody looking over my shoulder."

"The person I want you to spend time with is not in our business. He's a person I've heard about for many years. Lately, I took the time to watch him in action. You have heard, of course, of Socrates."

"Socrates? The old guy that hangs out at the Lyceum. Students around him all the time. Very smart man. What's the point? He's not in sales."

"Darius, this Socrates is well known because he leads people to draw their own conclusions—not only students but merchants and money lenders and lawmakers. He makes a torch light up inside their heads. That's the method of Socrates. To lead people to a decision because—with his help—they see it's the right decision. They have a name for his method—Socratic."

"Are you saying I should learn a new method?"

"You, Darius, are going to learn the Socratic selling method."

I

TAKING A SOCRATIC APPROACH

Chapter One

Salespeople, Think about Change

WE ALL HAD A SALES PITCH

In 1960, I finished my tour of duty as a jet pilot with the U.S. Navy. I loved those four years. I enjoyed the company of the other pilots in the squadron. I loved flying off aircraft carriers and landing back on them. It was the only job I've had that I had to get right every time.

But that was over. I had to move on, get a civilian job. I was married, with a baby on the way.

Richardson-Vicks had a great training program, so I made that company a target. A friend there got me an interview. Three days and seven interviews later, I was one of 35 salesmen (no women then) hired to cover the United States.

My assignment was to sell Vicks products to all the drugstores in New York City and Westchester County. I was supplied with a list of accounts: addresses, buyers' names, what they bought last year, even a suggested increase over last year's order. I was expected to make 12 calls per day, 60 calls per week.

I was trained to deliver a sales pitch: "How do you do, Mr. Jones. I'm with the Vicks company. We're making our annual call to offer you special discounts on fast-selling Vicks products for delivery in the fall. "Based on my analysis of what you ordered last year and your low inventory [I had checked the store room], I would recommend the special drop shipment number one deal, which provides you an 8.3 percent discount." Then I would show him on a deal sheet the products and quantities. The sales pitch ended this way: "All that for only $742, instead of $803, if you bought it piecemeal. As you know, we can ship it direct to you, but bill it through your wholesaler so that he doesn't feel we're going around him. What wholesaler would you like to use?"

That's the way I was taught to sell. Convince the buyer. I talk; the buyer listens. As time went by, I sold to wholesalers' chains, grocery buyers, department stores. Years later, I went into the advertising business. That was a big change—from selling products the customer could sniff, rub on, or swallow to selling a service that generated ideas about products. But one thing remained constant. I talked because I knew more than the customer. I knew features and benefits. I knew types of deals. I was good at talking, and back then I thought talking was what the job called for.

IS TALKING WHAT THE JOB CALLS FOR?

A few years ago, my company surveyed nearly 300 experienced salespeople, ages 31 to 45. Among other questions, we asked, "What is the number one problem among salespeople?" Here are the results:

Talk too much	41%
Overpromise on product performance	30
Fail to follow through on delivery	16
Other	13

We asked the same question of over 400 buyers nationwide. Very similar results, with talking too much again in first place. All these years since I sold cold remedies and advertising, and talking is still number one!

If I talked too much in front of customers, there had to be something I wasn't doing. After all, it wasn't like talking into a tape recorder. There was a person there. I know that because most of the time I was talking, I recall looking at somebody. There had to be a deficit on the other side of my talking.

THE OTHER SIDE OF TOO MUCH TALKING IS NOT LISTENING

I was calling on a pharmacist named Barry Bernstein on Fordham Road in the Bronx. He was complaining that our medimist nasal spray didn't sell. As he talked, I was trying to think of how to handle his complaint. It didn't require a major rebuttal, just a convenient answer.

When he stopped I said, "Well, Mr. Bernstein, I can take the medimist back and give you credit for them." He was surprised. He said, "Wait a minute; you just agreed with my point that if I displayed the bottles next to the counter, they would move. You were nodding as I said that." "Yes, of course," I said. But I hadn't heard him suggest relocating the display. I wasn't listening. I was thinking about what to say next.

I had made an error and I knew Mr. Bernstein caught it. It was the type of error that went with a busy job: 12 calls per day, with driving time and searching for a parking space between calls—average call, 30 minutes. Often the owner was busy and I had to wait. Forms to fill out, display pieces to put up, shelf facings to improve—little time and I felt it.

I could make a case for not taking the time to listen.

Back then, many salespeople would make the same case. With so little time with the customer, you had to make sure your products and services were discussed to best advantage. Customers typically didn't know as much as the salesperson. They would latch onto some problem that had an easy solution—like Barry Bernstein and the nasal spray. As customers talked, they used up your time. Talking time meant selling time. Every minute spent listening was a minute you weren't selling. That was the way I saw it.

I was not alone. Every salesperson I knew felt that the customer needed to be educated, and that meant the customer should do the listening, not us.

If, after all these years, talking too much is still the practice of salespeople, is it the same with listening?

SALESPEOPLE DON'T LISTEN

Not very long ago I was talking with a prospective buyer at an investment banking company. When I asked the buyer how his company's salespeople identified the needs of their clients, he responded:

> "It doesn't matter. We're not interested, because we already know what's best. We tell them what they need. I guess you could say we're opinionated."

I could have agreed with his guess, but of course I didn't.

Many salespeople today would admit to being opinionated, meaning that they know the customer's business and know better than the customer how they can improve it. If not listening is what you might expect in the fast-paced arena of financial sales, you can hear the same from sales managers in the crop-chemical industry, in places as far from Wall Street as Calgary, Alberta; Clovis, California; and Middleton, Wisconsin. I remember hearing the sales managers responsible for wholesaling to farm supply outlets describe their salespeople. Sample quotes from these sales managers:

> "Our reps are too busy remembering what they're going to say next instead of listening."
> "Retailers ask me why my reps aren't interested in hearing about the retailers' businesses."
> "Our reps just keep trying to force it down the retailers' throats."

Sales managers and buyers in a wide variety of companies say the same.

So, talking too much and not listening are still part of selling. Is this surprising? Not if you consider that for many years these practices were observed and labeled, but not rejected by the customer. No force emerged to make salespeople do the job differently.

SALESPEOPLE LIVE UP TO EXPECTATIONS

The image of the talkative salesperson has long been a cliché. The degree to which talking too much has been a nuisance to customers covers the spectrum. At one end you had customers who felt they didn't know much and were willing to sit through the sales pitch to learn about the product or service. At the other end were savvy customers who found the talkative salesperson a nuisance but made the purchase anyway. They got what they needed and avoided the ordeal of listening to another salesperson. Many customers saw in all that talk the salesperson's qualification for the job. People figured that if young Johnny had the gift of the gab, he belonged in sales.

Even those charged with raising the corporate image of salespeople by education and training had to bow before reality: sales made the business world go round and many salespeople who sold the old way were getting the job done. Nobody who could sell quota was fired for not listening to customers in the process.

The more corporations educated salespeople, the more salespeople could find reason to think they knew more than the customers. In recent years large numbers of technical people have been drafted into the ranks of salespeople. Their very expertise puts them at risk of believing that they should be talking and the customer listening.

ONLY CUSTOMERS CAN MAKE
SALESPEOPLE CHANGE

For something to change, the marketplace would have to change. And it has. As corporations compete today, new responsibilities are thrust upon buyers, and buyers respond with a new set of needs, skills, and expectations. Today's buyer doesn't want to be talked at. Today's buyer wants to be heard.

The salesperson who got by, or even became successful, by talking and not listening, will not succeed with this new customer. Today's salesperson needs to learn who this new customer is.

Chapter Two

Careful, This Is a Lion

A LION IS STILL A LION

From time to time a zookeeper gets mauled. Sometimes it's a lion tamer at a circus performance. The newspaper story always sets the event in a context of routine duties: the zookeeper was feeding the lion or sweeping out the cage; the lion tamer was going through the act. The story usually omits a clear cause of the attack. The reader concludes something was taken for granted, and suddenly the huge potential for disaster was realized.

The newspaper never does give the lion's side of the story. In terms of animal sensitivity, who could say? At the circus performance, was it a coincidence of flashbulb, the crash of cymbals, and an unaccustomed movement of the lion tamer? With the zookeeper was it the combination of a step closer and a back turned? Powerful animals frequently have a shot at their keepers—it's not really clear why they take it some times and not at others. The moral of the newspaper story is that when power is close, you can't take anything for granted.

When I was an account executive with J. Walter Thompson, I worked at headquarters in Manhattan. The president of this internationally known agency would often be seen about the building. You might meet him in the hallway or in any of the departments. He would chat with you at a coffee urn. He might drop into a meeting. A colleague used to say, "No matter how many times you see the president, he's still the president. A lion is still a lion."

That's right, the familiarity of a face can lead you to miss the reality: A company president has great power. The danger in performing routine duties with or around powerful people is that you take something for granted, your awareness of their power decreases, and you take your eye off the reality.

IN THE WORLD OF SELLING, THE CUSTOMER IS THE LION

As I added years to my experience in selling, I realized that in the world of the selling, the customer is the lion. It's not so much the president of your company as your customers you think of as having the power. The sale depends on the customer's decision. Your success in a sales career depends on a long series of favorable decisions by customers. No, the customer's perception of you is not to be taken for granted. You must sustain your awareness of customer power; otherwise—for reasons that you don't expect and may not understand—the potential for disaster is realized.

To balance the confidence that came of experience, I needed an occasional reminder: this is a lion, this is a lion, this is a lion. Because I believed that salespeople must talk—early and often—and because I believed that time spent listening was an undesirable deduction from selling time, I had no internal reminders, no warning signals that I might be taking too much for granted, that I might be losing awareness. The reminder came from without: no sale. Sometimes it came abruptly—I thought I would get the sale and instead got mauled. No sale is an effective reminder that the customer is powerful. Said *no* to me! What a lion.

Dealing with the customer is not getting easier. One of our customers put it succinctly: "The buyers are getting smarter faster than the sellers." Technology has changed the business world, and it has changed the buyer's role.

TODAY'S BUYER IS BETTER INFORMED

Back then, a druggist had a hard time with inventory. I used to go into Barry Bernstein's storeroom and find products that had dried up in the bottles. Today, even retail buyers have electronic access to information. Within moments they know what's in the back of the store or on a loading dock in warehouse or factory. They know the previous deals and their profits on those deals. They know who the providers are and some of the deals those providers offer.

In today's corporation, many buyers are a key source of information to the rest of the company. The buyer's knowledge contributes to recordkeeping and inventory control. Buyers attend trade shows and conventions, where they network within their industry—and outside it. Corporate buyers know what's coming on the market; they know what options and customized editions are about to become standard and thereby advance the product.

Buyers of services have access to a multiplicity of publications. They attend seminars and come away with videotapes that effectively showcase a service. You can see the increasing knowledge of buyers from the questions they ask: about credit options, physical packaging, marketing help or publicity to support their purchase, designated deliverers of a service, customization, scheduled modifications or improvements, alternative features, user education, guarantees, extended warranty.

Because of their knowledge, today's buyer is no longer merely a conduit from the decision maker to the supplier. The buyer is a key part of the decision-making process.

TODAY'S BUYER IS MORE ACCOUNTABLE

Back then, corporate buyers could hide bad decisions. Large organizations had those store rooms, figuratively speaking, where people could nap their way through a career and hide their mistakes there, too. Improved management practices have done away with much of that. Now buyers are visible. Good purchases and bad purchases are part of the performance portfolio.

The buyer has more at stake than the seller. If the purchase is a product and it dies, there's a body. To get rid of the corpse, you have to write it off. The write-off is visible on the books, and no comptroller will forget the page. Every mistake has a culprit. Every culprit has a name.

If it's a service that doesn't work, the buyer's purchase is a failure to those who participate in that service. Any degree of contact with the service entitles the victim to ask rhetorical questions of every other person in sight: Whose idea was this new information network? What made Hal think this direct mail set-up was any better than the old one? Couldn't Ellen see that this building layout wouldn't work for us? And so the buyer is reminded: wrong choice.

Back then, a retail buyer like Barry Bernstein could make inventory errors and still get by. Today, mistakes will get a retailer's windows boarded up. From the biggest customer to the smallest, there's a lot at stake.

WHAT'S NEEDED IS DIALOGUE

Dialogue is needed because a dialogue is, first, a purposeful discussion. The sales process brings together two people, each with a purpose that will be better defined in the dialogue itself. Besides clarifying goals, a dialogue refines the information that each party contributes. The customer and salesperson each bring a key asset to the process: the customer knows the history and needs of the organization. The salesperson knows the potential of certain products or services to give that customer a solution.

Not any kind of dialogue will suffice to fuse these assets into a solution. The dialogue needs a defined method with a record of success.

Chapter Three

This Method Makes Both Players Win

WHAT IS THE SOCRATIC METHOD?

I first heard of Socrates in high school. I can recall the teacher saying that even though we as teenagers had accumulated a vast store of knowledge and already knew 97 percent of all the answers anyone could possibly need in life, we ought to touch base with the great minds of ancient times. Okay, maybe this once, I thought. What I recall learning about Socrates in high school is that he lived in Athens about 400 B.C., had been a soldier, and became famous as a philosopher. Something else that stuck—and it's not surprising that it would impress a high school kid—was that Socrates was considered great company. Socrates had a sense of fun and attracted a crowd wherever he was.

A few years later I was in college and no doubt had edged a few percentage points closer to knowing all the answers. What then impressed me was a teaching method used by one of the professors. He preferred not to stand up there and lecture because that was just *telling* us, he said. He would get us talking until we arrived at a conclusion that was right. The method drew the answers out of us. He called it the method of Socrates—there was that name again!

Socrates left no writings. His dialogues were purposeful discussions on issues of the day. They took place in public and the method became well known—so well known, in fact, that decades after my schoolroom education, I could find the "Socratic method" no farther away than a dictionary. Here's the definition from *Webster's New World Dictionary*:

> **So̱ crat'ic̱ meth'od: A method of teaching or discussion, as used by Socrates, in which one asks a series of easily answered questions that inevitably lead the answerer to a logical conclusion . . .**[1]

Given the typical weaknesses in salesperson-customer dialogue, the potential for a Socratic approach to selling is enormous. The Socratic method treats the other party in a dialogue deferentially. Socrates' approach is attentive to the other party's perceptions. It is as if the other party were a lion. There is a realization that the case cannot be forced, but rather that much is to be gained by enlisting the lion's power.

SOCRATIC PRINCIPLE 1: RESPECT THE CUSTOMER

Respect is due the customer because the customer *represents access to another world.* In a sales dialogue the salesperson is an outsider, trying to gain entry to the world of the customer. That world is a culture with a value system of its own. Corporate customers often exhibit pride in the entities they serve and seem eager to explain the company's culture, vision, and mission.

As you speak to the customer, you realize how the mission of the company is seen through the perspective of the one or of the few employees you're with. This one person or small group of persons will quickly convert the corporate mission to a more manageable application. The world you and the customer talk about

---

[1] © 1994 with permission of the publisher, Prentice-Hall General Reference, a division of Simon & Schuster.

is a departmental responsibility or individual goal. Still an out-sider, you see a large organization on a smaller scale. You have entered a world more individualized.

In retail sales, the sales dialogue brings the salesperson into an even smaller and more private world. It's not so much the Rose Hill Pharmacy on Fordham Road as Barry Bernstein's store. Indeed, many salespeople who sell store to store are impressed with the individuality of the customer. Many salespeople actually sit down in the living rooms of their customers. The smaller and more individualized the site, the more the salesperson resembles a guest.

Outsiders Need to Be More Aware

To be a guest demands that you intensify your awareness. If you don't usually wipe your feet on entering your own living space, you remember to do so entering another's home. When you're a guest, your eyes and ears work harder at taking in the surround-ings. You get your bearings. If you have young children along, you watch their every move. The good guest is careful of damage and wary of giving offense. Increased awareness of where you are is an appropriate response to another's environment. The host takes it as a form of respect.

As a salesperson entering into the world of the customer, you have to step up your awareness. Not to be fully aware in the sales dialogue kills the dialogue. The typical mistakes salespeople make in dialogue are lapses of awareness. Salespeople who talk too much, ask the wrong questions, and don't hear what the cus-tomer says are distracted in the lion's presence. Their lack of re-spect for that reality increases the potential for disaster.

In the Socratic approach, the dialogue is built upon respect for the other party. The key idea for Socrates was that the dialogue was shaped by the answers given to his questions. Socratic selling respects the customer by taking each answer seriously. Unless the information coming from the customer is taken into account, the dialogue cannot continue.

SOCRATIC PRINCIPLE 2: HELP THE CUSTOMER THINK

The reason you must help the customer think is that the customer is a source of information. A source is not an agent. Nothing happens until you access the source and draw out the information.

The Socratic approach uses two closely connected dialogue tools: easily answered questions and full-value listening to the customer's answers.

1. **Easily answered questions** are a hallmark of the Socratic method. They are the great facilitators. They appeal to mind and heart. Socratic questions are easy to understand and always in the customer's interest to answer.

Easily answered questions suit today's customers who are awash in information. Information pours in through E-mail and V-mail and modem and conference calls and meetings and overflows the in-box. With the right questions, salespeople can make it easier for customers to sort out what they know.

If customers fail to think through and sort out their needs, they will buy what doesn't fit—a failure that costs both the salesperson and the customer. Fail they will, if the salesperson does not have the tools to help. Communication is that difficult.

2. **Full-value listening** means crediting the customer's answers to your questions with the impact those answers have as information. To begin with, you must understand the customer and must demonstrate that understanding. Every time you show you grasp a thought or idea expressed by the customer, the dialogue advances.

If you and I are having a friendly chat and I am using Socratic listening in our conversation—call it a dialogue—what you say counts. If you say what I don't want you to say, I can't pretend I didn't hear it. If you say what I wasn't expecting you to say, I can't bypass it and go on to the next thing I was planning to say. Socratic dialogues do not follow a script. In the Socratic dialogue, you are my partner. I may ask most of the questions, as Socrates did, but each of your answers is a necessary step on the way to a "logical conclusion."

SOCRATIC PRINCIPLE 3: HELP THE CUSTOMER MAKE DECISIONS

The Socratic process generates a series of logical conclusions that shape the sale. The sales dialogue does not take the customer's buying decision as one big yes or no. The approach goes step by step, through a series of decisions made by the customer.

For those decisions to be made, salesperson and customer need a clear-headed dialogue. Keeping it clear is the salesperson's job. Gradually, the customer concludes that you know the customer's business and that you can be trusted to work in the customer's interest.

Those conclusions lead to a final conclusion—to buy from you because it makes sense to do so. The outcome is a result of the integrity of the process.

The end result is progress for the customer. The customer's world moves ahead. Your product or service creates the brighter day. Both players win. Customers who feel they have been professionally treated will return. Even if the sale is for once in a lifetime, the customer will return in the shoes of others that customer sends to you.

II

OPENING THE SALE SOCRATICALLY

Chapter Four

It's the Customer's Meeting

AT THE OUTSET, THERE'S TENSION

You have arranged a meeting with a customer, usually by phone. So there are the two of you—or the seven or eight of you—because the customer may have brought a few others and you may have brought a boss or a colleague. For now let's say the two of you.

If the customer is a prospect, a stranger, there's tension. You don't know each other. There's nothing to go on but the agreed-upon topic of the meeting, and even that may be general.

If the customer is a regular customer, there's still tension. Tension? Why, I play golf with Larry, says the salesperson. Sharon and I are volunteers at the senior center, says the salesperson. Well, which is worse, dealing with a stranger and not getting the account at all or dealing with a familiar face and seeing some of the old business slip away to a competitor, or—horror—losing the account? Golf or volunteer work is not how Larry and Sharon make a living. Even as you now find the small talk easier, you and the other party feel the probing undercurrent of all business: whether the exchange of values important to each party will take place this time around.

THE TYPICAL OPENERS

Salespeople want to get on comfortable ground. How do salespeople try to get there quickly? Thousands of salespeople have
been asked how they begin a meeting. They tell us there are three
ways:

1. Begin with a sales presentation.
2. Begin by talking about your company and its products.
3. Begin by asking questions.

Typical Opener 1: A Sales Presentation

This is a prepared talk, usually aided by charts or the projection
of visuals or by a demonstration of the product itself.

Call it a presentation or a pitch or a dog-and-pony show, salespeople value the opportunity to stand up in front of a customer,
because it isn't easy to get there. You compete with other salespeople for the customer's time. Getting face-to-face with a customer is a main event. So why not make the most of the event?
Grab and hold the customer's attention with something the customer can see.

Beginning with a sales presentation is comfortable ground for
salespeople. The topic is what the customer asked for. Sure, the
customer ends up hearing a lot more besides, but customers
expect that to happen.

The presentation may be the company's stock presentation,
packaged by marketing experts and graphics specialists, not a
word of it the salesperson's. Another kind of presentation may
combine the wisdom of the sales force. Or it may be the salesperson's own creation, authorized by a sales manager. In one
way or another, the company stands behind the salesperson's
presentation.

Finally, you can let the charts and electronic props do part of
the job for you—all the better if it's the latest technology.

All of that is fine for the salesperson. Now take it from the customer's perspective. The meeting begins with the salesperson

talking about the salesperson. The graphics serve to underline that fact. The customer certainly didn't have a hand in their creation.

I'm not knocking sales presentations. For 25 years my colleagues and I have trained people in sales presentations. We have told people that to stand out you need to stand up. We believe that skilled organization and delivery make the presentation a powerful sales tool. None of that changes the point being made here. The point here is that if the meeting begins with a presentation, it begins with the salesperson talking about the salesperson.

Typical Opener 2: Talking about Products

This approach can be very comfortable for the salesperson because it is less formal, does not require equipment, and so is not liable to equipment breakdowns. Anyone who has ever had the equipment fill the room with smoke can see an advantage in not having any. Furthermore, both parties are seated, and you can hand brochures to the customer. Sliding glossy papers on the veneer of an expensive table is an acceptable substitute for foot tapping. It discharges nervous energy. It also allows you to break eye contact with the lion.

For the customer's take, it is still the salesperson talking about the salesperson. This version of the salesperson talking about the salesperson lacks entertainment value—no colorful bar charts, no high-tech line graphs, no pictures. If a picture is worth a thousand words, the customer is now getting the thousand words.

Typical Opener 3: Asking Targeted Questions

Ostensibly, asking questions is an effort to get the customer to speak and become involved. The questions, however, tend to be directed beams of light. They focus on those parts of the customer's world that the salesperson can tie into a salesperson's product or service.

The salesperson is comfortable because the questions control the way the customer becomes involved in the discussion. The focus of the question limits what the customer can say. Short answers by the customer ration the time allotted to the meeting, so the salesperson aims for short answers. For the salesperson, the meeting begins predictably.

For the customer, the handful of targeted questions is a peremptory way of dealing with the realities of the customer's world. The questions seem to extract information in nuggets. Is that *all* you want?, the customer might ask. What about the rest?

Although the customer does get to speak, the questions put the salesperson in charge. As a buyer in the field of information technology puts it: "I feel pressure when questions are thrown at me out of context. I don't like being sold to that way." Questions that seem out of context sound more important than the customer's answers could possibly be. The salesperson is really using questions to talk about the salesperson. That's how the meeting begins.

IN THE CUSTOMER'S MIND THE MEETING IS ABOUT THE CUSTOMER

Beginning the meeting in a way that puts the salesperson in control overlooks a reality: In the customer's mind, the meeting is about the customer. If there is any doubt why the customer thinks the meeting is about the customer, consider who the customer is.

THE CUSTOMER IS IN CHARGE

The customer agreed to the meeting, and by that consent, makes the meeting exist. In trying so hard to encourage new salespeople to set up sales meetings, let nobody forget who makes it happen. Salespeople can only knock on doors. They don't open them; the one in charge does.

Besides consenting to the meeting, the customer also consents to its topic, the time and date, and how many minutes you get. There's no doubt who's in charge.

In the reality of the sales meeting, the customer is the higher being. It's the customer's turf. The customer knows who determines the outcome of the meeting: whether there will be a second meeting and ultimately whether business goes on the books.

THE CUSTOMER WANTS TO SPEAK

Speaking defines what happens at a meeting. Customers, then, establish the lines of authority in the meeting by speaking. To let their authority be known, customers want to speak. *And they want to speak at the outset.*

Who's first in command? The customer.
Who goes first? The customer.

Otherwise, things get turned around at the outset. The person in charge is, in effect, made to be quiet and to listen and to answer when asked a question.

Some customers are regular buyers; others are strangers. Although professional backgrounds of buyers may have similarities within an industry, personalities can vary widely. How can you be sure the customer wants to talk? Besides having authority over the meeting, what else would make the customer want to speak?

THE CUSTOMER HAS THE INFORMATION

The customer has another reason for speaking. By speaking, the customer fills the information void created by your presence. No matter how much you know about the customer's world, the customer knows you don't know enough.

How can it be that you don't know enough, when much of your selling is to the same customers? The answer is under your nose. You can look at the drivers that are changing your own business: technology, narrowing profit margins, overnight competition. Those same drivers are changing the customer's business. What the customer saw as critical last time may not be so today. The world revolves more rapidly. The customer's perspective keeps changing.

Unless the customer sees you making an effort to understand that perspective, the customer sees you as self-serving. As an outsider, you are knocking on the door with your mind packed with guesses, eager to act on a set of assumptions that bypasses the most reliable source of information—the customer.

YOU NEED A WAY INTO THE CUSTOMER'S WORLD

Yes, your products and services might help the customer's world go forward—that's a view the customer shares—but at the moment of entry to that process, the customer sees you as unprepared and unequipped. You must first remove that perception and then gain the cooperation of the one person who makes the sale happen.

The difficulty of entering the customer's world is gigantic. Many salespeople try to break through at the outset without an effective method. Without a method for beginning, approaching this lion has potential for disaster.

Chapter Five

Begin Where the Customer Begins

THE LION TAKES IN THE SCENE

After the handshake and exchange of amenities, it may seem that some customers don't want to talk. Customers have a way of sitting back in thoughtful silence. If the customer has a perspective and wants to express it, why doesn't the customer do so? Why no roar from this lion?

Two reasons: one, the customer does not want to seem eager to buy. The first statements made in the meeting—after the small talk—are signals about the business at hand. Both parties sense that. In setting up the meeting, you and the customer discussed some topic, however general. By immediately reintroducing that topic, the customer may indeed seem eager to buy.

Second, the meeting was arranged so that the salesperson would bring potentially valuable ideas to the customer's attention. There's a professional expectation: You have asked for my time, salesperson. You have it. Now show me your magic.

Undoubtedly, these two reasons, not wanting to seem eager to buy and the professional responsibility of the salesperson to justify the meeting, are factors at the outset.

Despite these factors, the customer's self-perception remains the same. The customer is still the authority and information source. Not for a moment do these two factors diminish the customer's desire to be heard from. They do make themselves felt by ruffling the lion's fur at the outset. The lion must deal with these factors. The lion is tense at the outset because the lion wants to roar but senses it's not strategic. We've all seen footage of the lion in the bush, silently taking in the scene.

Something has to happen to make this meeting go right, and it's up to you to make it happen.

MAKE THE MEETING A SOCRATIC DIALOGUE

Begin with a Socratic opener. Here's an example:

Mr. Jones, I'm prepared to talk about _____, which we discussed on the phone. If you could give me your perspective on that, we can focus the meeting on what interests you.

The Socratic opener is not casual. Let's examine the elements. There are three:

1. Say You Are Prepared

"I'm prepared to talk about _____."

By stating that you are prepared to talk about your product or service, you show that you are responsible. You asked for the meeting and so built an expectation in the customer's mind. You're now telling the customer you've done what is necessary to meet that expectation.

By acting responsibly, you begin to establish your credibility. Your readiness to begin the meeting provides security for the customer. At the outset the customer is not put on the spot, doesn't have to risk anything, doesn't have to say a word, or do a thing. The meeting is in your professional hands.

Other ways to say you are prepared:

"I'm ready to discuss . . ."
"I'm here to tell you about . . ."
"I could start by explaining . . ."
"I have thought about the subject we discussed . . ."

Whatever the words, they must convey that you're ready to speak. Your readiness removes both factors that silence the customer: the avoidance of seeming eager to buy and the professional expectation that the salesperson make good.

2. Invite the Customer to Speak

"I'm prepared to talk about _____ , which we discussed on the phone. If you could give me your perspective on that . . ."

Note the choice of the word *perspective*. It's a *mind* word. Like *outlook, viewpoint, ideas,* and *thoughts,* the word *perspective* is about the *workings of the customer's mind.* Thoughts are the product the mind generates all day long. Everybody has a perspective, a viewpoint, thoughts on a subject, and is only too happy to share them. Because thoughts are invisible, they pass unappreciated. Rarely do others ask to hear about them.

Avoid words that are about the customer's *gut: problems, concerns, needs.* Later, the dialogue may get to gut. At the outset you haven't earned the right to get into anything even remotely emotional. And attributing needs to the customer may be presumptuous. "Wait a minute," the customer may say, "I didn't say I needed anything."

The choice of words is important:

Yes	Maybe	No
perspective	priorities	problems
viewpoint	goals	concerns
outlook	objectives	needs
overview	strategies	
thoughts		
ideas		

The "maybe" category is applicable if the customer has identified priorities and goals in a prior discussion. You may not assume that any objectives are in play. A customer might choose to see you simply because your subject is timely or interesting.

Not just to speak, but to speak on subject!   Note also that you invite the customer to speak *on subject.* Inviting a customer to "tell me about your business" is a roll of the dice. You could get 20 minutes of career history unconnected to the business of the moment. You can't risk having a digressive monologue use up the time.

How narrowly must you focus the subject? You are committed to helping the customer think. Following up on the conversation that set up the meeting makes it easy for the customer to begin. If the customer prefers to introduce a different topic, the dialogue will still be where it ought to be.

3. Offer an Immediate Benefit

*"I'm prepared to talk about _____ , which we discussed on the phone. If you could give me your perspective on that, **we can focus the meeting on what interests you.**"*

You are offering the customer an immediate benefit, not the benefit of your product or service—you're not there yet. This benefit is a sensible and productive use of the customer's time in the meeting. The benefit is right now. The benefit is logical and appealing because it connects the customer's mind with the customer's wristwatch: The meeting will address a subject of interest to the customer. What better use of the time?

Again, the words can vary, but the *you* in "what interests you" is strategic. Not "what interests us." Yes, the meeting will benefit the salesperson, also. Both of you benefit. So you could say, "Focus the meeting on what benefits us." But don't. The lion is accustomed to the lion's share.

THE SOCRATIC OPENER IS AN EASILY ANSWERED QUESTION

In using a Socratic opener, you are asking a question that can be answered easily. In its shortest form, the question would be: "What's your perspective on _____?" The customer has already considered the subject. The customer's answer can assume any form: brief or lengthy, detailed or summarized. Truly, the answer is easy.

But remember how the lion takes in the scene: unwilling to seem eager to buy and expecting the salesperson to deliver some magic. You just can't walk in, shake hands, and ask, "What's your outlook on _____?" The preparation—invitation—benefit formula is necessary.

The Socratic opener works best when it has been rehearsed out loud. Try practicing with a colleague. It's one thing to think about what you'll say—quite another to train the mouth to say the words you choose. Rehearsal guarantees that your mouth will follow your mind's orders. Rehearsal also helps you find your own best words. You can put together a toolbox with three or four of your favorite Socratic openers.

THE POWER OF THE CUSTOMER'S PERSPECTIVE

Some years ago, I had a meeting with the new chairman and CEO of a major fabric company. I had met him (call him Frank), but he was never the buyer. The old chairman (call him Bill) ran this company like a benevolent dictator. We had an active business relationship, but he had retired.

I arrived at the reception area at 10:45 A.M. for an 11:00 A.M. meeting. Eleven o'clock came and went. I began to get nervous. At 11:15, Frank, the new chairman, bolted through the reception room door. He was in shirt sleeves, sleeves rolled up. "Kevin, I'm sorry about the time, but I'm into something big and it concerns this whole company. I've got 15 minutes. I don't know if you want to reschedule this, or what."

Now the book says that a salesperson in this situation should say, "Frank, if the time isn't right for you now, why don't we get out our calendars and schedule a time when we can do justice to this subject." Then the prospect feels relieved and even in-debted to the salesperson. The next meeting ends up being more successful.

Did I do it by the book? Well, the book also says something about a bird in hand. I said, "Frank, I think the time is now. We'll do the best we can with the 15 minutes." We went into Frank's office. He sat behind his big desk, looked at me, and said, "Okay, Kevin, shoot."

I had rehearsed a Socratic opener, but saw those 15 minutes going pretty fast if he started to talk. Just to my left was my desktop presentation kit. On those charts was the presentation I had pre-pared for Frank. My hand twitched. It wanted so badly to begin flipping those charts.

I went with the Socratic opener: "Frank, I'm prepared to tell you about selling skills training. But here I am with the new chairman of this great company. You have a vantage point on this subject I'm not privy to. If you would share that perspective with me before I begin, I think we can make the next 15 minutes fairly hum."

Frank leaned back and said, "Kevin, you're used to selling to Bill. He ran the company top down. We're not running the com-pany that way anymore. Each of the 15 divisions of this company is run by a general manager. Any training we do will be decided by those 15 people. If I loved what you had to tell me about training, it wouldn't make any difference. You have to sell those 15 people."

Frank paused for a breath. Maybe it wasn't too late for my flip-charts! My hand was still twitching. Yet . . . the customer was unveiling his point of view.

"Here's what I'll do, Kevin. Every three weeks all 15 general managers attend an Operations Committee Meeting. I'll sched-ule you for one of those meetings. I'll introduce you to the man-agers, but it's up to you to sell them."

My hand was still twitching. It still wanted to turn those flip-charts and help me sell the chairman. But, as I sat there listening,

I realized he had presented me with an opportunity far beyond what I could generate for myself. I lacked the knowledge and the power to get in front of those 15 buyers. More than a tangible selling opportunity, I gained insight into how strong a customer's desire is to share a perspective. The 15-minute meeting lasted one hour. For 10 minutes of that, I spoke. For 50 minutes, Frank spoke. I never did get to the charts.

THE SCOPE OF THE CUSTOMER'S PERSPECTIVE

The aim of the Socratic opener is to provide a basis for a dialogue. Focusing the customer on the subject does not mean the customer won't speak on another subject. Another subject is okay. When a customer consciously broadens the scope of discussion to another subject, you might even be better off. Socratic openers generate some bountiful surprises.

If the response is surprising, it's because the Socratic opener invites a perspective. Perspectives are dynamic and changeable. Some years ago, a salesperson named Dan had been working with a pharmaceutical lab. Dan had received a letter from the Vice President of Human Resources. The letter itemized what a team of VP's were interested in addressing. Dan went to the meeting prepared to address those issues:

> Ladies and gentlemen, I'm ready to talk about the goals you've set for expanding the training of your managers. If you could fill out the picture as you see it, we can keep the meeting on what's important to you.

"Fill out the picture" was the catalyst for discussion. As it turned out, there was little match between the picture in the letter and the customers' perspective of the moment. Talking about the customers' picture led to a huge sales training endeavor that doubled Dan's business and revitalized the customer's sales force.

THE IMPORTANCE OF THE CUSTOMER'S PERSPECTIVE

The value to customers of expressing their perspective is seen in an experience of a West Coast salesperson named Jan. Jan met with 10 people from a major computer manufacturer. The meeting was to go 45 minutes. Jan gave her Socratic opener, and the customers talked for 40 minutes. When Jan, who was taking notes, glanced at her watch, they said, "Don't worry about the time, Jan. It's important that you understand us, and that's why we're taking the time to give this information."

Jan's meeting went 90 minutes, twice the allotted time, and led to a sale and a productive business relationship. Many, many users of the Socratic opener speak of similar experiences. Customers find patches of time as long as they can use it to express what's important to them. The Socratic opener makes customers make the time.

THE CUSTOMER DRAWS THE FIRST LOGICAL CONCLUSION

When customers are able to help salespeople understand them, customers conclude that *the meeting has been about the customer.* To the customer that means the priorities are in order.

The Socratic opener can lead the customer to a number of other conclusions: that you handle your responsibility for the meeting professionally, that you get the meeting off to a good start, that you respect the customer's time. You grow in the customer's esteem. Esteem generates trust, and trust is critical to a sales relationship.

A relationship takes time, but with a Socratic opener you go a long way in the first fifteen seconds.

SOCRATIC SKILLS NOTEBOOK

Begin with a Socratic opener:

1. Say you are prepared.

   "Mr. Jones, I'm prepared to talk about _____, which we discussed on the phone . . ."

2. Invite the customer to speak on subject.

   "If you could give me your perspective on that . . ."

3. Offer an immediate benefit.

   "We can focus the meeting on what interests you."

Every customer has a perspective on a subject and is only too happy to share it. Ask.

Chapter Six

Help the Customer Tell the Need Story

THE NEED STORY IS ABOUT YESTERDAY

Once the Socratic opener invites the customer to speak on subject and the customer accepts the invitation to share a viewpoint, you are going to get a perspective. The camera pans back, taking in the near past. To tell you how it is now, the customer tells the story of what led up to now.

The customer goes back in time because that's where the need is. That's where the facts are. Knowledge of the need is a report on yesterday:

> "Our maintenance system for our fleet of trucks is costly and inadequate."

That statement obviously covers a few months if not a few years. "Is not adequate" took time to get that way. The present is just the cork holding in the past. Sometimes the cork explodes out of the bottle; other times the contents pour out quietly.

THE CUSTOMER OWNS YESTERDAY

The past is full of the customer's successes and mistakes. It's full of the customer's decisions and rescinded decisions. If the customer is unlucky, the past is a history of wise endeavors thwarted by other forces. Maybe the customer's wise wish list was torn up and discarded by a committee. It's all there in the customer's mind. The customer knows the story behind the statement: "Our maintenance system for our fleet of trucks is costly and inadequate."

Whether this customer let the system become inadequate, or somebody else did, this customer is now saddled with it. That's the beauty of the past; it belongs to the customer. It's the customer who can best interpret it. It's the customer who must mend it. The customer owns the past.

THE SALESPERSON'S EYE IS ON TOMORROW

Now let's insert a salesperson in the middle of this customer's perspective: a large fleet of trucks that are breaking down, with costs escalating out of control. The salesperson is looking in a different direction. The salesperson is looking only to the future.

That's because the sale is in the future, and you are expected to get there. The training expended on salespeople is future-oriented. You are force-fed product knowledge. You have to know how the products and services should and would work for the customer. You are taught the features that distinguish your products or services from one another: this one basic; that one enhanced. You are drilled in the inner workings that give your product an edge over a competitor's. Following the grand design from headquarters, you can explain its advantages and answer the customer's questions. What sales manager would trust you with a customer if you couldn't? Learning about the product is learning how to position it, explain it, defend it, and, of course, sell it. All of that looks to the future.

To the salesperson it makes sense to talk about where you want to go and what you want to do: "What I can do for you is . . ." or "What you ought to do is . . ." The salesperson is selling a promise.

The customer may think about the future but does not want to visit it—not right away. Ready or not, the salesperson pushes the customer into the future. As the self-designated "opinionated" salesperson said, "We're not interested in hearing what they need. We tell them."

Quickly forced into the future, which the customer neither owns nor knows, the customer cannot do justice to the past by thinking it through with the salesperson's help.

HELP THE CUSTOMER THINK ABOUT THE NEED

The Socratic opener helps at the outset. Customers talk for varying lengths of time after the Socratic opener. Because the customer's input must be taken seriously—that's the Socratic process—you want to help the customer do justice to the story. To ensure that the need story is told, set these objectives:

- Draw out all information the customer sees as part of the need.

- Access possible areas of need the customer does not see.

- Create a picture that satisfies both of you.

ASK EASILY ANSWERED QUESTIONS

A principal Socratic tool for reaching those three objectives is the easily answered question. The easily answered question helps the customer think—for these reasons:

- The question yields control of the dialogue to the customer. The customer is free to go this way or that with the reply. No barrier of defense is thrown up against the question because it doesn't come *at* the customer. On the contrary it draws the customer to move toward the salesperson.

• The easily answered question is relevant to the need picture being drawn by the customer. The question always advances the dialogue; it never distracts the customer.

USE SOCRATIC PROBES

Many types of "easily answered" Socratic questions fit the purpose of the dialogue. "Socratic probes" are very useful at the outset of the dialogue. The aim of the Socratic probe is to increase the volume of information from the customer. Ideally, during the exploration of the need, the customer should be talking 80 percent of the time; you, 20 percent.

Socratic "Draw" Probes

Once a topic is on the table, the Socratic method draws on the customer's reservoir of information. Socratic draw probes lock onto a topic and keep drawing until customer and salesperson are satisfied with the results. Here are some Socratic draw probes:

Tell me more about . . .
Would you elaborate on . . .
Give me an example of . . .
What else should I know about . . .
What else would help me understand . . .

Look upon the Socratic draw probe as having a probing-listening structure. The front end invites a flow of information in whatever way the customer wants to tell the story—a few words or many. The back end shows you've been listening to the last few points touched on by the customer. If you were talking with a VP of sales about the sales force, you might use the front end–back end structure as follows:

Probing (front end)	Listening (back end)
"Tell me more about . . .	. . . the strengths of your sales force."
"Would you elaborate on . . .	. . . the maturity of your salespeople?"
"Could you give me an example of . . .	. . . how you train salespeople?"
	. . . the causes of turnover?"
	. . . teamwork among your salespeople?"

The words *strengths, maturity, train, turnover, teamwork*, show you have been tracking with the customer's input to the dialogue.

The Socratic probes, of course, fit any topic in a dialogue about needs:

"What else should I know about . . .	. . . your mission?"
"What else would help me understand . . .	. . . your role?"
	. . . your department?"
	. . . your relationship to the R&D function?"
	. . . your responsibility for quality control?"

In the example below, note how the probes not only draw out more information, they also show that the salesperson has been listening.

In this dialogue the salesperson represents a truck maintenance corporation. The customer represents a manufacturer with a large fleet of delivery trucks.

Salesperson:

Fred, you have talked about a number of maintenance problems causing your operating costs to escalate. **Tell me more about** your vehicle breakdowns.

Customer:

We have trucks leaving on a 1,500-mile round trip when they're overdue for tune-up. That part's our fault. We don't have the personnel to oversee preventive maintenance. The other part is that some of our drivers aren't good at spotting something wrong. They bring in a tandem that's sure to have a problem with both the tractor and trailer when it goes back out.

Salesperson:

Can you elaborate on some of the tractor-trailer problems the drivers don't tell you about?

Customer:

With the tractor it's transmission. With the trailer it's the underside: tires, shocks . . .

Using these probes, this salesperson will hear what there is to know about the need. It takes some patience, especially when you hear details from one customer that other customers in the same industry have described to you. It's not yet the time to sell into the need—not before the need is finished. Socratic probing requires self-discipline.

Believe that the sale is being made during the discovery process. Not one moment is wasted when the customer is speaking about the need. Your ability to handle this process will weigh heavily in your favor later in the dialogue.

Socratic Probes Give You a Running Start

These Socratic draw probes—"Tell me more about . . .," "What else should I know about . . .," and their equivalents in other words—are not only easy for the customer to answer. They are easy for the salesperson to *ask*.

The front end of the probe is a ready-made verbal tool: "Tell me more about . . ./What else should I know about? . . ." If the front end of the question is in place, you have a running start. You don't have to think of how to phrase the question. Questions are energy burners. They don't come to mind perfectly formulated. The more you can reach for ready-made questioning tools, the less you are distracted by the effort to use questions.

Ready-made questions also help you to concentrate on the customer. Many salespeople try to think up questions that impress the buyer. They spend thinking time on that next intelligent question and miss what the customer is saying. An important part of the need story slips by.

GAIN ACCESS TO WHAT'S MISSING

Help the customer think is the second principle of the Socratic approach. After your Socratic opener has invited up-to-date perspectives, your draw probes help the customer give you information. But you may not hear all that's worth hearing. The customer is not using a checklist and may forget a particular need or simply not realize that an issue is important. Some customers who know the general need—for example, to insure the corporation against risk—may not know all the particular issues that should be discussed.

Once again, help the customer think. If the picture is incomplete, use questions that give you access to what is missing. Before meeting with the customer, make a list of topics that may touch upon the customer's needs. Some general topics, for example, are productivity, inventory, competition, equipment, communications, teamwork, safety, and morale. The more you know about the customer's business, the more specific your list can be.

COMPLETE THE PICTURE WITH
SOCRATIC ACCESS PROBES

To gain access to topics that may fit into the need picture, use the Socratic approach. Your probes should allow the customer to think freely about the fresh topic and say whatever comes to mind. Here are some examples of Socratic "access" probes:

How does _____ fit into the picture?

Talk to me about _____ .

How do you handle _____ ?

Continuing the dialogue, the salesperson asks about a topic that the customer hasn't included in the description of fleet maintenance problems:

Salesperson:

How does refueling fit into your picture of fleet maintenance?

Customer:

Right now, we leave it to the drivers. We're not set up to handle it ourselves. But refueling at truck stops is costly. It's one of the reasons the cost of operating the fleet is getting out of control.

From experience in selling truck maintenance programs, this salesperson has many ideas about making truck maintenance operations cost-effective. Refueling services is one of those ideas. It's a subject that has to be covered.

Socratic Access Probes "Bring Ideas to Light"

Some commentators on the Socratic approach call the process one of "bringing ideas to light." The customer wants to talk about ways of making truck maintenance cost-effective. A refueling program is an idea that fits the picture, but for the customer the refueling idea remains out of sight. The salesperson helps the customer think. The access probe "How does refueling fit into your picture?" brings the idea to light.

Other ideas related to fleet maintenance may require more explanation by the salesperson—for example, vehicle washing or a safety program for the fleet's drivers. An alert and responsible salesperson isn't going to sell a two-part maintenance program when the customer could benefit from a five-part program. The difference between the alert salesperson and the intrusive or insistent salesperson is in the questioning and the listening. The alert salesperson searches for a piece of the picture that seems to be missing. In so doing the salesperson recognizes that it's the customer's picture. If the customer doesn't want that piece in the picture, a salesperson using the Socratic approach will respect the customer's wish.

The Socratic probes are tools that encourage the customer to share a unique viewpoint and to take 80 percent of the dialogue time, if necessary, to develop that viewpoint.

You are now familiar with three dialogue tools:

- The Socratic opener.
- Socratic draw probes.
- Socratic access probes.

The world of the customer is large, and information about needs is found in its many corners. Certainly, you need more tools. They will be presented in Part III.

THE CUSTOMER REACHES TWO MORE LOGICAL CONCLUSIONS

1. **You're looking in the right place.** When Socratic questioning follows the invitation to talk on subject, the customer senses that need knowledge is being sought where it is to be found. Right here, with *me*, thinks the customer. Here's a salesperson who's looking in the right place! And the past, which the customer owns and knows so well, is given its due. The customer feels no premature push toward the future and its many decisions.

2. **You made good on your promise.** If your questioning helps the customer think, and in no way obstructs the flow of information, you and the customer will arrive at a clear understanding

of the needs. Such an achievement makes good on the promise of your Socratic opener: to make the customer's time worthwhile.

When do you get to the end of the need story? After minutes, hours, or a number of days. Pharmaceutical lab reps who sell directly to physicians measure the call in minutes. For most salespeople it takes a large part of one meeting, if not a series of meetings. For those who handle trusts and estates, the meetings may be spread over years. If you follow the Socratic process, the customer will tell you when you've reached the end.

However long it takes to finish the needs story, the customer feels: so far, so good.

SOCRATIC SKILLS NOTEBOOK

The customer owns the past.

The customer has no stake in the future—until the past has been dealt with.

Help the customer tell the story.

1. Use Socratic draw probes:
   - *"Tell me more about . . ."*
   - *"Would you elaborate on . . ."*
   - *"Give me an example of . . ."*
   - *"What else should I know about . . ."*
   - *"What else would help me understand . . ."*

2. Use Socratic access probes:
   - *"How does _____ fit the picture?"*
   - *"Talk to me about your experience with _____ ."*
   - *"How do you handle _____ ?"*

Believe that the sale is being made when the customer speaks about the need. Not one moment is wasted.

III

ADVANCING THE SALE SOCRATICALLY

Chapter Seven

Find Out Why Now

THE CLOCK ALWAYS RUNS ON THE SALESPERSON

You can't fly to a meeting in another city without being impressed with the demands of clock and calendar. First, you estimate how long it takes to get to the airport. At the airport you are met with dozens of monitors showing departure times. Departure times are deadlines with minideadlines called boarding time. Once you are on board and in the air, the pilot announces the expected arrival time. Be thankful if you have no connecting flight, or you will think about that deadline flying halfway across the country. You pull out the airline magazine and flip through inserts advertising project organizers and day keepers. For years the airline magazines have sprouted foldout ads or tear-off coupons related to managing one's time. The ads and coupons wouldn't be there, month after month, were not clock and calendar terrorizing business people in general and salespeople more than most.

Salespeople are always selling against time. Typical sales careers are punctuated with annual quotas for revenue generated and quarterly quotas for new product sales. You sell into limited-time promotions. You strive to persuade a prospect to move ahead on a purchase before a competitor steps in and whisks away the business.

GETTING THERE MAKES THE CLOCK RUN FASTER

Travel adds unique complications to the time factor. Most sales-people don't get the job done in their offices. Travel throws them up against airline delays, traffic snarls, and unforeseen physical barriers like a fallen tree on the tracks of a commuter line.

On one occasion I entered the lobby of my customer's building with five minutes to spare before a 10:00 A.M. meeting. The elevator started up—and stopped. The half dozen people on the elevator groaned. Two men in shirtsleeves were probably returning to their offices. Two fellows in biker's gear were making deliveries. A woman who might have been making a sales call shook her head and looked at the floor. I looked up at the lighted panel that displays the company situated on each floor. There was my customer's company, on the 15th floor. Here was I somewhere in the shaft. Ten o'clock went by . . . 10:05, 10:10. From somewhere above us a voice called down the shaft, Don't worry, don't worry. I wasn't worried about my life; I was worried about my sales call. Eventually, building maintenance workers got the elevator up to the next floor. I was 35 minutes late for the call.

THE CLOCK RUNS FASTER ON THE CUSTOMER

In the 35 minutes I waited in that elevator, customers were taking care of their needs in a timely fashion. Customers on the floors above and below that elevator, customers in the adjacent buildings, and customers throughout the city were buying what they couldn't wait any longer to buy. Microchip manufacturers were buying silicon. Computer manufacturers were buying microchips. Computer companies were buying microchip companies. And they all were buying advertising services and marketing services and banking services and human resource services. The pressure of clock and calendar against need is driving all of these sales.

Salespeople may tend to picture the customer as someone not pressured to see a salesperson. You get to believe it's tough to see a customer because they are busy doing their job. Their job is the priority. Seeing a salesperson is something the customer slips in between legitimate job activities.

A salesperson whom I had just congratulated for his break-through year in sales surprised me by saying he found it very hard to increase the number of weekly sales calls. Phone calls, he felt, interrupted a customer's workday. At a certain point in the day or week, his desire to pick up the phone and ask for a meeting began to weaken. But for that, he said, his sales could have gone beyond that year's achievement.

THE BUYER NEEDS YOU NOW

As your energy for the sales effort ebbs and flows, think about how much the customer needs you. Part of the customer's workday is to pursue solutions that can be found only by purchasing products or services. The customer needs to know about you. If you don't take the customer's time, some other salesperson will.

What if you turned the sales situation around and looked at clock and calendar from the customer's vantage point? When time is a factor, a growing degree of urgency wraps itself around the process of making a decision to buy. The customer feels no relief from the urgency because there's no alternative to the deadline. The only latitude the customer has is in choosing the seller of whatever is needed to meet the deadline.

DEADLINES CREATE URGENCY

In corporate selling, those deadlines fall into five categories.

1. Seasonal Deadlines: The Calendar Tells You When

There's no mystery to seasonal deadlines. It's all there on the wall calendar. The deadline dates are not so much the work of decision-makers as predetermined by holidays, annual events, and the rotation of the seasons. In the great chain of seasonal buying, Valentine's Day chocolates, Easter bonnets, patio furniture, back-to-school kits, and ski outfits move mountains of goods from manufacturers to end user. The change of seasons drives needs in the farm, tourist, and construction industries. The calendar is integral to the product or service. Not many jackets with fur-lined hoods get sold in June.

2. Phase Completion Deadlines: They're Predictable

Each year corporations develop plans that specify long-range goals. At designated dates certain phases of development must be completed. Each department in the company reaches for resources to accomplish those goals. Each decision to use outside resources follows the project's advance on a time line. If your buyer keeps you advised on developments, you are able to be a player at the crucial junctures in the time line. A relationship with the customer gives you great advantage over those who depend on general sources of news about the corporation.

3. Start-Up Deadlines: They Mean Get Moving

Seasonal deadlines and phase completion deadlines are there for all to see. Some less visible factors create pressure on the buyer. A start-up deadline is one. Corporate energy is fitful. Response to markets or shifts in strategy may call for projects to be launched suddenly. A need is perceived. An executive or operations or management committee decrees that action be taken. Task teams investigate solutions. Ideas are bounced upstairs, back downstairs, and then sideways. A decision is made to find an outside resource.

The pursuit of a solution is handed to a person or persons who are your potential customers. Their need is to *act*. Their need is to *get started*—in the sense of: get the ball rolling, get moving on this project, get it on its feet, forge ahead. Lurking behind the upbeat metaphors are their shadowy counterparts: stop dragging your feet, get off the dime, don't let this get dust on it, move your butt.

Customers are human. Like everyone else, they get stuck in internal meetings and are delayed by the procrastination of others. They wait too long to interview salespeople. Dust does get on it.

The urgency wraps around the customer's need to make a credible decision: a decision to go with you or somebody else. If you can encourage the customer to talk about that urgency as part of a perspective, you have reached need knowledge that is a priority to the customer. Strange as it may seem, the customer's first need is to be perceived as getting started on a solution. The second need is the solution.

4. New Broom Deadlines: Act before New Gets Old

Another type of time urgency applies to a buyer who has just come into a position of authority. This so-called new broom may sweep out the current products and services. New brooms like a new look. I remember an executive who took over responsibility for corporate advertising and, just like that, fired an ad agency that had handled the company for 50 years. In its place he hired four boutiques agencies—a great upheaval! Change, even upheaval, is expected of new brooms, and they are granted powers accordingly. Change is costly, so with those powers goes a budget for new products and services.

Look for new brooms to act fast. The optimum time for new bosses to expand floor space, upgrade equipment, and introduce new services is at the beginning. The longer new brooms are in the job, the more likely their designs for innovation will slide into the ordinary channels of budget. Be alert to their need to take advantage of the moment.

5. Unspent Budget Deadlines: Not Spending Carries a Penalty

One of my strangest experiences as a Navy pilot was firing 20-millimeter shells at the Atlantic Ocean. Each year the Navy would take inventory of jet fighter ammunition before submitting a budget to the Pentagon on June 30. To the Navy, an ammunition surplus in peacetime would jeopardize its next year's budget. To make sure the surplus was expended, twice a day during June we took off in squadron from our base in Virginia, flew to a designated area of the ocean, and raked the waves.

You might think that in the private sector unspent budgets are channeled into corporate profits. It doesn't always happen that way. Departments may have unspent budgets, which become another less visible kind of time urgency for the buyer. Spending the budget becomes a need in itself. The departmental buyer is in a bind: don't spend the surplus and be cut back on next year's budget, or spend it unwisely and be held accountable. You can help the customer apply the surplus where it can be productive.

ASK EASILY ANSWERED QUESTIONS ABOUT URGENCY

Using the Socratic process, help the customer think in terms of time and urgency. In answering the Socratic questions, the customer connects needs to the influence of time. The dialogue advances.

Why is action important at this time?
Why now?
What makes this urgent?

Why are you thinking of this now? Two answers:

- Because all eyes are watching for something to happen now.
- Because if the first steps are not taken, the project falls too far behind.

In this dialogue the customer is a corporate benefits manager, and the salesperson is a consultant representing a benefits consulting group.

Salesperson:

Alice, you've given me a description of your current benefits plan and why senior management considers it too expensive. *What makes it urgent to change right now?*

Customer:

Three months ago top management decided we should take a different approach. I had a number of meetings with the HR boss and someone from finance. I showed them how the discussions weren't addressing the inefficiencies in the old plan. Then they backed off and left me with the whole thing.

Salesperson:

So there was motion in one direction and a stop. Now you have to get started in a new direction.

Customer:

I have to do it fast. The employees have the feeling that the benefits plan is being kicked back and forth. The employees also feel that no matter what we come up with, they get you-know-what done to them.

Salesperson:

Sounds like it's important for them to see something happen right now, with results not far off.

Customer:
> Absolutely. The results need to be in place in months. Nobody at any level in this corporation wants to hear "next year" talk.

URGENCY INFLUENCES THE CLOSE

When time urgency is a part of the need picture, it has an impact on closing. The greater the time urgency in the need, the more advantage you have in closing. That advantage depends on the customer's experience of the urgency in the sales dialogue. Some customers may miss it. Others may find the urgency unpleasant to deal with.

By pursuing Why now? you invite the customer to confront the urgency. If the customer makes the time urgency a conscious part of needs awareness, urgency will carry through the sales discussion, through your proposal, and be a factor in closing.

THE CUSTOMER REACHES A LOGICAL CONCLUSION ABOUT URGENCY

An experience that never fails to bond people is a race against time. Time is everybody's diminishing resource. So many goals are not reached because too much time is lost at the outset—no time to catch up. Then someone helps the customer get it going. Together, two people collaborate on racing successfully to the finish. Those two people can be customer and salesperson. **Those two people can be this customer and you.**

SOCRATIC SKILLS NOTEBOOK

The clock runs faster on the customer.

Ask easily answered questions about urgency.

- *"Why now?"*
- *"What makes this urgent?"*
- *"Why is this important right now?"*

Take advantage of the highly visible deadlines.

- Seasonal deadlines
- Phase completion deadlines

Watch for the less visible deadlines.

- Start-up deadlines
- New broom deadlines
- Unspent budget deadlines

The customer's second need is a solution.
The customer's first need is to get started on a solution.

Chapter Eight

Let Feelings Drive
the Sale

FACTS ABOUT THE NEED DETERMINE
CHOICE OF PRODUCT OR SERVICE

The Socratic process helps the customer think through the need. The customer sorts out many facts and fills out the picture for you. Your Socratic probes encourage a flow of detail that eventually will help match the need with your product or service.

The process goes beyond facts. Awareness on the part of the salesperson is key to respect for the customer. An aware salesperson will pick up another level of information, that of the customer's feelings about the need. Everything the customer communicates in the dialogue must be taken into account, and so the customer's feelings are a valuable part of the dialogue.

THE CUSTOMER'S FEELINGS
DETERMINE THE BUYING DECISION

The buyer personalizes the buying decision by investing feeling in it. To some, such an assertion is surprising. In their personal lives salespeople would readily admit to feelings about the purchase of a house, a car, or a gift to a loved one, and perhaps also about an article of clothing, a vacation trip, or an object used for a hobby. But in the corporate world feelings might seem at first to be no factor at all. The very decorum of the corporate world itself—dress code, neatly contoured properties, subdued interiors—would suggest objectivity, analysis, fairness, balance, measured judgment.

All of those attributes belong in a corporation, of course, but any significant corporate purchase is layered with human feeling. You run smack into feeling just by defining the elements of the corporate purchase:

The customer or buyer	Somebody accountable for purchases.
The need	An aggregate of circumstances not acceptable to the buyer and the buyer's company.
The product or service	Also known as the Right Choice or the Wrong Choice.
The investment of the buying entity	Heaps of money and time and the reputations of persons involved.
The selling agent or company	Either a stranger, a familiar face who doesn't always deliver, or an old reliable who does.

Now, is there feeling here or is there not?

The feelings that personalize the buying decision can be looked at as if on three levels: irritants, motivators, and relationships based on trust.

As real as feelings are for those who experience them, feelings are harder for other parties to identify. To get an idea of feelings a customer may have, picture a traditional house. It has a basement, a ground floor, and an upstairs floor. Let's picture it as a neighbor's house: you get to visit it occasionally, much as you as salesperson call upon your customer occasionally.

THE BASEMENT LEVEL OF FEELINGS: IRRITANTS

In the basement of your neighbor's house, there are no secrets. Basements hold back nothing. Everything is in sight; nothing is tidy. Dad's tools overflow the workbench. Clothing overflows the laundry hampers over there by the kitty litter. The kids' toys cover the floor. Somebody flushes a toilet upstairs and pipes gurgle inches above your head. The boiler rumbles. In winter it can be very warm down there! What goes on in the basement leaps at your eyes, ears, nose, and skin.

You might say "irritants" are basement feelings. They're not tidy. The customer doesn't hold them back—not much, anyway. They tend to overflow, and when they do you can feel the heat.

The customer's irritant feelings come in two categories:

Irritant 1—The Burned Buyer Irritant

When your Socratic opener or Socratic probing uncovers dissatisfaction with business done with another salesperson, you can foresee a change in the buying pattern. Being burned by the other company is part of the story.

Customer:

> I was guaranteed a shipment of 5,000 compressed air cylinders. It doesn't show up. My boss says, "Where are they?" I say, "I don't know." My boss says, "Well, you better find them. Maybe by this afternoon you can find 100. Maybe by tonight you'll find a thousand. Then maybe you can find the other 4,000 tomorrow, so this plant can stay open."

Salesperson:

> That's a frustrating situation to be in with your boss.

Customer:

> You can say that again! Here my boss is about to blow his top, and I look like I can't do my job.

Salesperson:

Yes, you take a hit because somebody else doesn't deliver on a promise.

Customer:

Try to explain that to anybody at the plant—they don't care. They just want the shipment.

Salesperson:

What did you say to that supplier?

Customer:

When I got him on the phone, I told him . . .

Let the Customer Re-Create the Experience

The burned customer relishes retelling the story because to the customer it cries to heaven for justice. Given the chance, the customer will keep talking. Let the customer go over the feeling. Let the irritant have its due. Pain is part of the picture and is attached to the need. And somebody else is the culprit.

The facts of the story—how a current supplier screwed up— are not the important element. It's over for that supplier; there's sure to be a change. That compressed air cylinder business is now up for grabs. You're just one of many candidates, and this isn't the moment to try to grab it.

Concentrate on the feelings in the story. You want to be taken back in time to the moment of the customer's hurt. Allow the customer's story to take you back so you can witness the personal cost to the customer of the supplier's mistake. For that reason draw out the story; encourage the customer to tell every detail. No salesperson who witnesses this customer's pain would ever let a thing like that happen again. And given the propensity of most salespeople not to listen, you'll probably be the only witness. The other salespeople this customer talks to will rush to offer guarantees that their company never misses delivery, which is what the original supplier did. No, the customer doesn't need to hear any more guarantees. The customer needs somebody to hear the pain.

Irritant 2—The Bleeding Wound Irritant

The bleeding wound irritant has nothing to do with a competitor's mistake. The bleeding wound is a situation the customer originally tolerated, hoping the negative circumstances would be resolved. The situation remains and the customer can bear it no longer.

In this dialogue, the customer is a manager of information systems for a corporation. The salesperson represents a computer software company.

Customer:

> In order to upgrade the information system I've been telling you about, top management wanted to form an operations analysis group. I hired a half-dozen analysts from the outside. We needed an elite group—we just didn't have the capacity on staff. What I ended up with are a half-dozen experts who don't agree with each other or anybody else.

Salesperson:

> So, your IS upgrade depends on internal consultants that don't play as a team. *What bothers you most about this situation?*

Customer:

> They are extremely particular about everything—hardware, software, you name it. They're slowing me down by arguing there are a zillion better ways to do everything in IS. Maybe so. I need one way. They use words like *nanosecond*, but it will take them till the end of the century to reach our objective.

Salesperson:

> You're saying they're so fussy *it's hard for you to move the project along.*

Customer:

> Exactly. They don't want a workable upgrade; they want a system to accommodate their potential—which they feel has no bounds.

Sure, they know more than I do, but they make every IS meeting twice as long and half as productive as it should be.

Salesperson:

You're talking about some costs here—the hours logged by six people aren't productive, and the project is wearing on you. You need a way to focus their expertise.

Customer:

If you could help me with that . . .

Instead of trying to transform the customer's feelings into an impersonal, rational analysis, the salesperson lets the feelings play out: The bleeding wound is part of the need picture. The salesperson will eventually become the physician of choice. Originally invited in as a software expert, this salesperson will partner with the manager in getting the elite consultants to work toward an objective.

ASK EASILY ANSWERED QUESTIONS ABOUT IRRITANTS

Once the customer discloses an irritant, these questions make it easy for the customer to relive the experience and develop the story in its painful detail. Without intruding on privacy, the probes invite the customer to elaborate on a subject that raises feelings.

What bothers you most about this?
I sense you're frustrated by this.
How tough a position does this put you in?

Some probes such as, "I sense you're frustrated by this," take the form of a comment. Not every probe has to be a question. Whatever invites the customer to express the feelings serves as a probe.

THE GROUND FLOOR LEVEL OF
FEELINGS: MOTIVATORS

Motivators are like the ground floor of the neighbor's house. You can't be sure what the ground floor looks like most of the time because it is cleaned or straightened up more often than any other part of the house. It's the busiest part of the house, yet it looks like nothing much happens there. You get the feeling a lot of things have been put away and covered up just before you rang the doorbell, and a few more just after you rang the doorbell.

Another thing about ground floors is that doors to the outside are always opening and closing. There's so much coming and going on the ground floor, it's hard to tell the true temperature of the place.

Now let's say you call on a corporate customer. As it is with the ground floor of a household, your corporate host straightens up the place for your visit. You don't see motivators at first. Motivators don't jump out at you the way irritants do. The feelings that motivate your corporate customers are not openly displayed. Like many things pertaining to a neighbor's ground floor, they appear in the open when you're not there, and then are put away.

If such feelings aren't obvious, do they exist? You can be sure motivation is real at the feeling level because business is so relentlessly competitive. Competition exists between individuals within a company, between groups within a company, and, of course, between companies.

Within the corporate world you visit, feelings generated by competitiveness may be whispered to a supporter at the water cooler, expressed to an opponent in an office confrontation, or even vented in a meeting. You're not present. To catch the feelings that motivate the customer, you have to be keenly aware. Stay aware, and you'll find the motivators.

Motivator 1 — Pressure on the Customer to Perform

As you use Socratic flow probes, you may find there's an aura of intensity surrounding the need. Some needs, once you have helped the customer describe them, don't so much call for satisfaction; they *demand* satisfaction. Such a need becomes attached to the buyer. You know the need and the buyer are handcuffed together when you hear that little clink:

> "I've been *stuck* with this situation . . ."
> "I can't just *sit on* this problem."
> "There's a *lot on the line* here."
> "The egg *hit the fan* last month when . . ."
> "I want to get this *off* my back."
> "There's a *lot riding on this* . . ."

In this dialogue the salesperson is in charge of sales and banquets for a hotel. The customer wants the right hotel for the corporation's annual convention.

Salesperson:

You've told me that check-in and dinner service are points of concern. *Please tell me how this affects you.*

Customer:

It's the timing. I can't fly everybody in between 3:00 and 5:00 so they can check in and be ready for the welcome reception at 6:30. We need some rooms ready at noon. One thing that turns it sour at the outset is a scene at the check-in counter when rooms are not ready.

Salesperson:

Beginning on a bright note is critical. Sour faces at check-in are certainly not something you should have to worry about. Your check-in needs should get close attention. You also mentioned dinner. *Tell me about the impact of that.*

Customer:

> Well, we've got 600 people. It's a hot meal and the last dozen tables shouldn't get it served cold. In a hotel the size of yours, kitchen and waiters can get out of sync. I don't want to be sitting nearby when that happens.

Salesperson:

> You're right. Everybody likes to hear a waiter say, "Careful, the plate is hot." And you need to be sure of that so you can direct your attention to the after-dinner events. The meal service needs to be carefully planned. *What other points of concern do you have?*

Customer:

> In particular, none. Timing overall needs a lot of thinking if I'm going to sleep nights until this thing is over with.

Salesperson:

> A plan for timing could govern the whole approach. I could show how hotel operations can be tailored to your schedule. Would that take some of the pressure off you?

Customer:

> It sure would. I'd like to go over that with you.

Do you think this salesperson will get the business? No question about the outcome—even though other hotels could meet those particular needs about room availability and meal service. The facts about those needs belong to every hotel sales rep this customer tells them to, and no doubt a few other hotel reps looking for this corporation's business have heard them. The feelings belong only to this customer, whose buying decision is personalized by pressure and concern.

This salesperson hears about the facts that pose problems, but is in no hurry to convert those facts into proposed solutions. Instead, the salesperson focuses on the impact these facts have as potential problems for the customer. The Socratic approach takes into account the buyer's feeling, recognizes it expressly in the dialogue, and accords it value.

For Some Customers Everything Is at Stake

Some customers feel the most painful of pressures: their job is at stake: "I've been pulled in by my boss. If I don't get this back on track . . ." Or the business they own is in trouble. They must produce a solution and they need to rely upon an outside resource.

If you begin with the Socratic process, you are committed to getting their perspective. You can't rush in with solutions until you understand the situation, no more than a doctor can write a prescription without examining the patient. Your questions will help them describe their precarious situation. In sharing a deep level of concern, they are forming a bond of trust with you. Whatever it is you sell that can help, products or services, these customers see them channeled through the trust they place in you.

Motivator 2—The Customer's Desire to Succeed

With pressure to perform goes fear of failure. On the other side is a positive surge of feeling: a desire to succeed. The customer's feelings may be buoyant—a project is under way, an initiative is launched, an opportunity comes around the corner. The customer is enthusiastic and wants to get it done right.

In this case the customer is a financial officer and the salesperson an investment banker.

Customer:

Since joining this company, I've always worked in the borrowing mode. I dealt with banks to get us enough to acquire some properties and pay some bills. Now we've just sold off a division. Suddenly, the people upstairs drop $20 million in my hands and tell me to invest it.

Salesperson:

That's having your hands full, Edith.

Customer:

It certainly is. Borrowing is something that became second nature to me. But I've never invested a dime of this company's money.

Salesperson:

How does this affect you?

Customer:

I see it as an opportunity out of the blue. When I came in here, I was the only woman in finance; later, the only woman involved in major decisions in any of the divisions. Now, they're saying to me, "We like what you've done; we trust you." I want to step up to this job and show what I can do.

After the topic of a career opportunity has been discussed, this salesperson will ask questions about the corporation's investment objectives—for example, parking the money short term, investing in a venture capital fund, and so on. Those are the questions investment bankers ask. Probably, most would not ask, "How does this affect you?" What relevance does such a question have to investment objectives? Directly, none. The question is first about the customer and her job, and second about the relationship between salesperson and customer.

This customer's motivation to handle a new role successfully influences the way she and the investment banker see each other. By asking, the salesperson is intelligently responding to the situation described. By answering, the customer is telling the salesperson how she wants to be seen.

See each customer as a person with a career and legitimate career ambitions, and see your product or service as a stepping stone for them. Salespeople who recognize their customers' opportunities know the whole need story. Make your customers look good and you will be invited back again and again.

ASK EASILY ANSWERED QUESTIONS ABOUT MOTIVATORS

With motivators, the issues are personalized either as pressure to perform or opportunity to be a star. But motivators are not as evident as irritants. This is the ground floor, remember. There's a lot of coming and going. The customer's feelings get lost in the routine recital of facts. Try these probes for motivators:

How does this affect you?
I sense this means a lot to you.
Why is this important to you?

These probes provide an opportunity for the customer to personalize the need. As easily answered questions, they contain no assumptions, nor do they intrude in any way. They invite the customer to tell the story at whatever level the feeling is experienced.

THE UPSTAIRS LEVEL OF FEELING IS TRUST

Only people who have gained a degree of trust—some relatives and some close friends—have access to all parts of a house. A pleasant thing about the upstairs of a house is the uniform temperature. With no doors to the outside opening and closing, heat circulates more evenly. It's like trust. The feeling of trust becomes a uniform basis for salesperson-customer relationships. Relationships generate initial sales. Relationships facilitate repeat business. Relationships allow easier access to the customer and give you the inside track against competition.

Most sales are closed through the feeling of trust the customer has in the salesperson. True, lower price is often a factor. The salesperson who says a competitor got the business because of lower price is very often right. But if the same salesperson builds trust through the Socratic approach, a competitor's lower price will have a weaker pull on the customer.

Remember that so-called sales advantages—such as added features or greater flexibility in the product or service, for example—are developed in the seller's world. These advantages are offered to the customer from outside the customer's world. Trust the customer feels in the gut. It begins there, grows there, and the customer knows exactly how it feels.

In some businesses you can easily see how much regular customers enjoy a sales relationship. They love to pick up the phone and start the process: "Mike, you want to do some business? Get out your book . . ." The lion likes to give that little roar.

THE CUSTOMER DRAWS A CONCLUSION ABOUT YOU

If the customer has personalized the need with you, discussed it at the gut level, then you have been taken into confidence. You are becoming an insider. Others—your competitors—may hear the facts, but only you have taken the time and made the effort to hear the whole story.

You know more, and because you know more you are now seen as better equipped to address the need. The customer has already begun to invest in you. Another stepping stone is in place.

SOCRATIC SKILLS NOTEBOOK

Facts about the need determine the choice of product or service.

The customer's feelings determine the buying decision.

Ask easily answered questions about feelings.

1. For irritants:
   - *"What bothers you most about this?"*
   - *"I sense you're frustrated by this . . ."*
   - *"How tough a position does this put you in?"*

2. For motivators:
   - *"How does this affect you?"*
   - *"I sense this means a lot to you."*
   - *"Why is this important to you?"*

Sales are closed through what the customer feels.

Chapter Nine

The Sharpest Competitive Edge Is Listening

IN A SOCRATIC DIALOGUE, YOU LISTEN

Listening to the customer is the most important asset you bring to the Socratic dialogue. Whose meeting is it? The customer's. Who is the key source of information? The customer. What happens to that information if the salesperson does not listen? It no longer retains its full value. It becomes fragmented. Uncertainty arises because the customer doesn't know which fragments are picked up and which are not.

THE CUSTOMER NEEDS TO KNOW YOU UNDERSTAND

Not to *know* you're understood can be acutely frustrating. It's an experience like that of a pilot "transmitting in the blind." The Navy has a procedure requiring a pilot to make radio transmissions to the tower, even if the pilot's radio can't pick up the tower's signal. I remember flying a Navy jet from Pensacola, Florida, to Oceana, Virginia, and hitting monstrous turbulence 35,000 feet over Atlanta. I was obliged to contact Atlanta air traffic control.

So I transmitted: "Navy Jet One Zero Five reporting in over Atlanta. Do you read?" Silence. No radio signal from Atlanta. I transmitted again. Silence. Five times I tried to reach Atlanta. No response. So I followed standard procedure, saying, "This is Navy Jet One Zero Five transmitting in the blind." I stated my position, altitude, and time over Atlanta station and estimated my arrival time over Raleigh-Durham, my next reporting point. What I remember most about the experience was the frustration of transmitting in the blind.

In a sales dialogue the customer is "transmitting" to a salesperson who is sitting a few feet away. Very often the signals coming back from the salesperson have nothing to do with the customer's transmission. The customer is talking about the past and the salesperson begins to talk about playing a role in the customer's future. The customer gets the unsettling feeling that the salesperson's input into the dialogue is a programmed signal. Regardless of the message the customer transmits, the salesperson stays with the program. There's no response.

The customer needs to know you hear. Think back to the promise of the Socratic opener: That the meeting will address what interests the customer. That the time will be well spent.

LISTENING FOSTERS LASTING RELATIONSHIPS

Relationships grow as customers perceive that you understand their world. The only way you can understand is to listen. Listening is being there with your mind, with your whole person. Understanding requires all the effort you can expend.

Once you begin to understand, you begin to be welcomed into that world. It's safe to have you there. Once you're inside, you belong. The relationship lasts.

As the relationship gathers momentum, it becomes efficient for you and the customer to work together. All your listening to the customer's prior needs creates a store of ready-to-apply information. The customer doesn't have to start over with a new listener.

LISTENING FOSTERS UNBEATABLE RELATIONSHIPS

Because you listen and understand, information transmitted to you generates a force. You can act in the customer's best interest. In a sense, you become a spokesperson: what the customer knows, you know. That's hard to beat.

As you repeat the experience of bringing solutions to the customer, you get better at it. It's difficult for a competitor to dislodge you as an insider. Does a competitor tout high-quality products or services? Do the competitor's products or services have some advantages over yours? If so, that matters, but how much does it matter? Nowadays quality is a necessity. The competitor's quality is seen from a distance. Your quality is that of an insider. Yours is seen up close. Listening got you close.

Does your competitor offer a lower price? Lower price will always capture individual sales. Lower price doesn't foster sales relationships, because price tends to become a condition of the relationship. Price goes up, customer goes away.

LISTENING IS THE SHARPEST COMPETITIVE EDGE

Competitive edges can be gained and lost. For example, a product or service you sell may enjoy brand name recognition by consumers. For you that's a competitive edge. But you won't retain that edge if a competitor's product overtakes yours in name recognition. The same can be said of other so-called edges.

If you are a skilled listener, you hold a competitive edge in winning and keeping customers. Is your practice of listening an edge you can lose to competition? It would be if competitors recognized the power of listening and sought to develop themselves as listeners. You might then have a competitive field on which most players used listening as a means of developing customer relationships.

Lucky for you, the listener, listening gets scant recognition by your fellow professionals. And because listening is not strongly identified with selling, listening remains the advantage of the few. Your secret is safe. You are not likely to be outlistened by competitive forces. The sharpest competitive edge is the one your competitors don't want.

In Promising, the Salesperson Has Plenty of Company

Listening and promising stand back-to-back in the present moment and step straight ahead, listening into the past and promising into the future. The future is where the salesperson's solution is delivered. You can't listen to the future. The future hasn't yet happened, so there's no story to hear. The future is the land of promises.

In sales, as in love, promises are necessary. Some sales promises are couched in intelligent and exciting proposals (see Chapter 11). The downside of promising in the sales dialogue is that the veteran buyer has heard promises by the thousands. Some salespeople walk in the door promising. Others just can't resist the smallest opportunity to guarantee the customer's future. Promising alone doesn't get the sale, and promising makes all salespeople sound alike.

Listening gives you the customer's story, with its facts and with its feelings created by urgency and irritants and pressure motivators and success motivators. Missing all that is not a good trade-off for whatever the salesperson gains by promising.

WHAT LISTENING IS NOT

Listening to the customer is sometimes confused with recognizing the connections between the customer's thoughts and your own. Here are two common examples of that error.

1. "Save Your Breath; I Already Know"

What you already know cannot be subtracted from what you need to hear. Forget the mathematics. Even if you know 50 percent of the customer's story, you need to hear 100 percent.

Customer:

> We are going through a major reorganization. Jim Brennan, our CEO for nearly 10 years, retired. Ned Paulson's in charge . . .

Salesperson:

> I know. I read about that in *The Wall Street Journal.*

What's the reaction to this misguided attempt to impress the customer? Does the customer think: *Hey, this salesperson is really on top of things! Good. Now I don't have to tell him very much. We can save 10 minutes.*

No, the customer's thoughts are these: *You know? What do you know? You're an outsider who knows what the press reports about my company. I'm an insider. The reorganization affects me, not you.*

Those thoughts never get to be words. They do their damage just flashing through the customer's mind. Even if you know everything the customer tells you, it's not the same as being told by the customer, because the information belongs to the customer psychologically. When you preempt the rest of the story, the customer's reaction is, Hold it. I'm the lion, not you.

2. "We'll Come Back to What You Were Saying after My Commercial"

Listening for cues in the customer's story to begin a pitch is another misguided way of connecting the customer's thoughts with the salesperson's.

Customer:

What our problem boils down to is that we lose a lot of time just getting merchandise in and out of this warehouse . . .

Salesperson:

Sounds like you'd love to get your hands on a bunch of these forklifts here in my catalog.

Well, why not, thinks the salesperson. There is a clear progression of ideas: warehouse to loading merchandise to forklift. In fact, a forklift may be a perfect solution. But the forklift is not part of the customer's story. The salesperson is butting in.

Listening is a mode of selling. For listening to function, other modes of selling, such as talking about products, must be switched off.

SOCRATIC LISTENING MEANS STAYING AWARE

Awareness enables your brain to gather the material content of what the customer says. You track with the information. The first time you are taken on a tour of the customer's world, awareness is easier. The story you're hearing is about a new company or a new industry. After selling often to the same customer, the story begins to sound familiar. Be careful of "Save your breath; I already know."

No matter how alike yesterday's customer and today's customer may sound, stay aware; stay awake. Every customer is unique. As close as one seems to another, the story each tells has a unique imprint.

To Stay Aware, Take Notes

Taking notes can help you remain aware. If it's a regular customer, don't just take notes on what's different this time around;

record what's the *same*. Customers like to see you write as they talk. It suggests the meeting is going as it should—the lion gets the attention.

Taking notes not only permits you to break eye contact with the customer, it *requires* that you look down at the page. If you are taking many notes, you should be looking more at your notepad than at the customer.

Consider the young salesperson who has been taught "Look 'em right in the eye" and scribbles furiously while looking right at the customer. What does the customer do? Breaks eye contact to look at the salesperson's notepad! Why? Because the customer wants to see how the salesperson could possibly write on the lines of a notepad without looking down.

SOCRATIC LISTENING GIVES FULL VALUE

Giving full value means you take into account everything the customer says. Selling a single product or an inflexible service may be a challenge to full-value listening. A salesperson may have to offer the product the way it's built, period. If the customer's need story presents a detail that doesn't fit the product, the salesperson may want to minimize the importance of what the customer says. Rather than give full value to the unwanted statement, the salesperson may pretend it was not said or see it as an objection and try to argue the information away.

Remember that you are selling solutions. Your product or service is a means to that end. A product or service that has little or no flexibility may satisfy a wide variety of needs. Consider how many consumers with unique needs buy the same product at a pharmacy or supermarket! The need of each is no less unique. Giving full value takes discipline and patience. Remember, the customer can make the sale happen; you can't.

YOU HAVEN'T LISTENED UNTIL YOU DEMONSTRATE YOU HAVE

The only way to demonstrate that you've listened is to "play back" to the customer what you've heard. There is no substitute for having the customer hear you say it. However, you must summarize rather than mechanically repeat content. You are not a tape recorder. A machine captures everything, replays everything, understands nothing. Your ability to summarize demonstrates understanding.

The customer gives you a message mixed with facts and feelings. Facts are thought to make up most of the fabric of information. Customers give you an array of facts, and without the facts you couldn't sell. Listening for facts can be difficult for some salespeople. As the customer's story accumulates facts, the salesperson has to store them in short-term memory. Eventually, too many facts crowd the memory shelf.

YOU CAN'T GO WRONG PLAYING BACK

Playing back may intimidate the salesperson who is afraid of failing the listening test. You should know that good things happen whenever you play back facts. If your playback shows a mistaken understanding of the facts, the customer is only too happy to correct the error.

Both of you benefit. You get a sharper view of the picture. The customer welcomes the opportunity to fix the picture. In fact, the customer loves being given the opportunity to set the record straight. How many salespeople have given this customer a chance to correct their misinterpretation of what the customer tells them?

If your playback shows you are tracking with the information, the customer is encouraged to keep talking and will add information to complete the picture.

CUSTOMER:

- **Corrects/Modifies:** . . . "No"/"Yes," but . . ."

  OR

- **Adds Information:** . . . ."Yes, and . . ."

  OR

- **Confirms:** . . . . "Yes."

DIALOGUE ADVANCES

In this dialogue, the customer manages marketing for a specialty foods chain. The salesperson sells telemarketing services.

Customer:

So my biggest need right now is to cut costs for marketing services. Our expenses are more than they should be.

The customer has been talking about the need to restructure existing marketing services.

Salesperson:

You want to spend less on the services you are currently using. Is that it?

This playback tries to clarify the customer's need before too many facts cloud the picture.

Customer:

Well, it's not so much spending less as getting full value for my dollar. For example, we have a lot of dedicated phone lines that we use full time. But many of our dedicated lines are used only part of the business day.

The customer corrects the salesperson by sharpening the focus of the picture. A Socratic dialogue typically corrects itself before errors waste time.

Salesperson:

In other words, you see yourself spending money to have something you don't use enough.

This playback shows that the salesperson now has it right.

Customer:

Yes, and we're thinking of adding four locations. That means more dedicated circuits. I'm afraid of repeating the same problem.

Note how naturally the playback draws more information. Most playbacks also have the effect of a draw probe.

Salesperson:

Let me go over this. You have many dedicated lines that are fully productive, but some that get only limited use. You would like to extend this marketing service to four new locations. Your concern, then, is how to do so and get better dollar value for what you are buying.

"Let me go over this" introduces a summary and signals the customer to check it carefully.

Customer:

That's it.

The customer agrees and, by not adding more information, signals the salesperson to direct the dialogue. The salesperson's options are to use Socratic access probes (Chapter 6), go for conditional decisions (Chapter 10), or make a proposal (Chapter 11).

PLAY BACK THE PERSON

The facts belong to the world. The same facts apply more or less to the situations of many customers, and not every fact is important. Feelings belong to individuals. What is important to the customer is tinged with feeling. If you listen carefully, you will catch these important statements. When you play back what is important to the customer, you are listening at a higher level of intensity. You are capturing the person of the customer.

In the dialogue below, the customer is a senior executive in a corporation. The salesperson is a broker.

Customer:

As you know, I've been with this company 30 years—company officer for 20. During that time I've had a significant amount of income. I put whatever I didn't need into securities—even took a flier now and then! Growth was what I was most interested in because my salary gave me what I needed to live well. Now, in three months, I retire. The salary stops. Sure, I get income, but not the same as before. So what I'm concerned about as I look at my retirement fund is where do I get that income? I've gotten used to it. I've got to be sure I re-arrange my assets to deliver it.

Salesperson:

Richard, you're saying you want more income from your investments.

Does that play back the person? No. The playback states very generally that Richard needs retirement income. Richard took 35 seconds to state he needed retirement income. Some of his person must have rubbed off on the story.

Let's identify each statement, separating the facts from the feelings:

Facts	*The person*
1. 30 years with the company.	
2. Significant income.	
3. Extra income into growth stocks.	
	4. Didn't have to worry about cash flow. It was there.
	5. Enjoyed living well.

6. Retires in three months.
7. Income not the same.

8. Concerned about retirement income.
9. Has gotten used to income/living well.
10. Must be sure assets deliver income.

How would this serve as a summary playback?

Richard, let me see if I have this. During your work years you had significant income. You lived well and what you didn't spend, you invested with no concern about cash flow. After you retire, you want to live the way you're accustomed to. So your concern now has changed. You want your assets to deliver enough income. Am I getting the picture?

Short and to the point of what interests the customer.

CHECK YOUR LISTENING WITH EASILY ANSWERED QUESTIONS

After you play back what you've heard, you should verify that your understanding is correct. Only the customer knows whether or not you have it. Some questions to check on your listening:

How does that sound?
Do I have it right?
Am I getting the picture?
Is that it?

THE CUSTOMER DRAWS AN UNUSUAL CONCLUSION

Listening shows you know the customer. That's the usual conclusion the customer draws from your ability to play back facts and, most important, to play back the person.

Customers draw another conclusion that seems to be a mirror image of the salesperson knowing the customer. Knower and person known are reversed. **When salespeople listen to customers, the customers feel they know the salespeople!**

This phenomenon occurs even when virtual strangers prove to be good listeners. Being listened to speeds up the knowing process. You do the talking, but you sense you're getting to know the listener. You get a sense of this happening when you are helped by attentive and helpful salespeople at retail counters. Watch for it also at social gatherings. Among the many people you meet for the first time, the good listener is the one you feel you got to know.

In reality, the customer may not know many facts about you, only data about your company and its products and services. But the customer has learned one significant attribute of yours—you are a good listener! **The customer concludes you are reliable and can be trusted. Listening lays the ground for a business relationship.**

SOCRATIC SKILLS NOTEBOOK

The sharpest competitive edge is the one your competitors neglect.

1. The customer needs to know you understand.
2. Listening fosters lasting relationships.
3. Listening fosters unbeatable relationships.

You haven't listened until you can show you have listened.

1. Play back a summary of the facts.
   - If you don't get it right, the customer is happy to help you try again.
   - A playback draws fresh information.
2. Play back the person.
   - Ask yourself, What is important to the customer?
   - If the customer has feelings about it, the person is involved.

Ask easily answered questions:

- *"How does that sound?"*
- *"Do I have it right?"*
- *"Am I getting the picture?"*
- *"Is that it?"*

When you play back what is important to the customer, you capture the person of the customer.

Chapter Ten

Get the Customer Started on Decisions

IT'S TIME FOR THE FUTURE

Customers understand themselves. They know the story they have to tell—about how things are in their world and how they got that way.

Customers may not understand how a salesperson's product or service fits into that understanding of their world and its needs. The customer does not know how to join the past and the future.

Thus far, you've helped the customer create a picture of the past and present. To create that picture, you used a Socratic opener, easily answered questions to help the flow of information, and easily answered questions that reveal urgency, irritants, and motivators. The picture of the customer's need is almost complete.

Now you have to help the customer broaden the horizon of the picture—to include solutions that bring progress. Help is on the way. The elements of this new picture will be decisions. Decisions begin to shape the future. Just as events are the brushstrokes in the picture of the past, decisions are the strokes that paint the future.

The customer must decide whether to buy from you. That's obvious. But first, the customer must make other decisions. Except for the simplest of transactions—a few coins get you a cup of coffee or a newspaper in a few seconds—the buying decision does not stand alone.

Your job is to help the customer think and make decisions.

WHAT DECISIONS DO YOU NEED TO KNOW ABOUT?

In his *Just-So Stories* written in 1902, Rudyard Kipling makes this rhyme about the tools of a journalist:

I keep six honest serving men

(They taught me all I knew.)

They were what, and why, and when,

And how and where and who.

Kipling believed that the answers to "what" and the other questions served him workable stories. As a journalist, he learned what he needed to know.

Those same questions can be turned toward the future. For your product or service to bring progress to this customer's world, which of those questions needs an answer? *Speaking to the customer*, what do *you*, the salesperson, need to ask?

1. **What** is it you want? That is, what kind of product or service in terms of model, features, applications, and so on.

2. **How many/How much** do you want? In other words, quantify your need for the product or service. Do you need this much or that much?

3. **When** is the product or service to be used? *When* can mean a date for start-up preparations, the date of implementation or delivery, or the effective date of a contract.

4. **How long/How often** is the product or service to be used? Duration and frequency.

5. **Who** is involved on your side? That includes decision-makers other than yourself and persons who would use the product or service.
6. **Where** is the product or service going to be delivered or used? How does location enter the picture?

Is every question necessary? No, only those questions relevant to your type of business and needed to fill in the picture. The question "What kind? . . ." is not needed if only one kind of a product or service could apply. The question "where?" is unnecessary if location has nothing to do with the solution you will offer to the customer.

HELP THE CUSTOMER MAKE DECISIONS

Why does the customer need help in making these decisions? These decisions are stepping stones to one big decision: "Yes, I'll do business with you. I'll transfer my company's assets to you in return for your promised solution. I'll buy your product or service."

People are afraid of making decisions. Unlike the past, the future can't be trusted. However messed up the past may have been, however needy the customer's organization may be, the problem with the past is at least known. Better the devil you know than the devil you don't. The future is uncertain. Today's customer is accountable more than ever. "I'll transfer my company's assets to you in return for your product or service, *but what if your product or service lets me down!*"

DECISIONS PUT PRESSURE ON THE CUSTOMER

The final decision the customer makes is "Yes, I'll do business with you." Two of the other decisions are so close to that final decision they raise the same anxiety. "When do you want to start with my product or service?" To the customer that creates nearly as much pressure as the final decision to do business. Time creates deadlines. "When" is an extremely sensitive decision.

Another is the quantifying question: "How many do you want?" or "How much do you need?" In other words, how big is the deal? That's getting close to the final decision. For the customer, uncomfortably close. The customer knows where those questions lead. They lead to "Yes, I'll do business." The customer may say, or think, "Slow down. You're pressuring me!" Customers who feel pressure are uncomfortable dealing with the future, and invariably they back away from decisions.

"IN DREAMS BEGINS RESPONSIBILITY"

The Irish poet William Butler Yeats wrote: "In dreams begins responsibility." What he meant was that if people imagine the future, they see themselves in it. They begin to have a role in it. Imagining the future leads one to have a stake in making the future happen, in shaping the way it happens. Responsibility comes fast on the heels of such a thought process.

By answering these questions the customer gradually takes responsibility. How can you make it easy for the customer to give those answers?

IT'S EASIER IF YOU SAY *IF*

Your questions need to remove pressure and remove risk. It's easier for the customer if your question is asked in a way that takes a "time out" from reality, that steps momentarily into fantasy, that says: What you answer doesn't count; it's only thinking out loud; it's only seeing with your imagination.

Make the decision conditional. Your easily answered question might look like this: "If you were to go ahead with this, when would you do so?" That is, *imagine* going ahead with a final decision. In that case, when would the product or service begin?

For the customer with the fleet of trucks, it could sound like this:

If you were to put your fleet into a maintenance program,	*when would you start?*
If you were to go ahead with the program,	*how many trucks would be serviced?*
If you were to decide on comprehensive maintenance,	*which locations would come under contract?*

As you can see, the front end of the question is a lead-in; the back end elicits a specific decision:

Lead-in	*Specific decision*
If you were to go ahead with . . .	**when** would you . . . **how many** would you . . . **where** would you . . . **what kind** would you . . . and so on.

FANTASY QUESTIONS ARE EASY TO ANSWER

You are asking questions that elicit information as far as you're concerned, but involve commitments for the customer. To be easily answered, the question must remove pressure and risk. Not just any wording of the question will do. Select a wording that actually helps the customer understand it's a "time out" from reality. Each question should have three fantasy components that achieve that.

Fantasy Component 1: Conditional Words

The question uses conditional words that assure the customer the decision "doesn't count."

If you were to go ahead with a
maintenance program . . .   *. . . when would you begin?*

If, were to, and *would* are conditional, pressure-free words.

Fantasy Component 2: Exclusion of the Salesperson

The question excludes the use of *I* and *we*. Only *you*—referring to the customer—enters into the formula:

If you were to decide on a
maintenance program . . .   *. . . which locations would you*
                                     bring under contract?

To some salespeople the exclusion of *I* seems like checking your gun at the door. In a sense that's what it is. Remember, you're sitting a few feet from the customer. You reduce the customer's sense of risk by assuming a low-profile vocabulary.

What good would it do to begin with *if* and then let yourself intrude verbally on the fantasy? Here's how it sounds the **wrong way:**

If I could get you to agree that
our truck maintenance program
is a good idea . . .   *. . . when could I get you to*
                               sign the contract?

If you let us take care of your
fleet . . .   *. . . how many vehicles will we*
                       be seeing each month?

Using *I, we,* and *our* assumes you're the only game in town. That assumption cancels the benefit of the conditional words.

Fantasy Component 3: Exclusion of the Product Name

The question never assumes that the customer had made a decision to buy. Therefore, exclude your company name or product/service name from the formula. Keep it neutral. Here's how it looks the **wrong way:**

If you go with our Happy
Trucks Service Program . . .   *. . . which of your locations*
                                        would come under the **Happy**
                                        Trucks Service contract?

Asking the customer to make a conditional decision attached to your brand name comes across as a transparent sales device. Your brand name creates even more pressure if the customer is using another service. Now two product names collide in the customer's mind! A question phrased as, "If you were to start a new maintenance program" is easier for the customer to handle.

CONGRATULATE THE DECISION MAKER

With every decision, a moment of truth is reached. The decision maker feels vulnerable. When you are dining out with family or friends, that moment of uncertainty about the menu arrives. After some discussion with the waiter and those at the table, you make a decision. The waiter says, "Good choice—you won't be disappointed." You feel relieved. You've heard that comment in dozens of restaurants. You feel relieved every time.

By the principles of the Socratic approach, you respect the customer, help the customer think, and help the customer make decisions. Once a decision is made, congratulate the customer. The customer's decision has just brought some progress into the world. Something is on the way to getting better.

SUPPORT THE DECISION MAKER

Recognize the decision and accord it full value. Show acceptance; shine a light on it.

You support the decision and the decision maker by playbacks and comments. Playbacks confirm understanding. Commenting on the decision shows acceptance; it's a way of saying amen, "so be it." Without your comments, your questions and the customer's conditional decisions are cut off from the rest of the dialogue. When you comment, all the dialogue elements—questions, answers, playbacks, comments—flow with the purpose of the dialogue.

Salesperson:

Fred, if you were to go ahead with a truck maintenance program, when would you begin?

Customer:

Probably in October.

Salesperson:

October. That's good. You'd have all your vehicles through one maintenance cycle before the holiday rush.

The salesperson's comment, "October," is an echo of the customer's decision. The echo is conversational and supportive. "That's good" is appropriate in this example, because the timing is favorable for the holidays. But you don't have to come up with the clever comments of a talk show host. If the customer's answer to your "when" question is "in two weeks," your comment can be, "Two weeks—that gets right on it!." You are saying, "So be it; thanks for the decision."

You may ask for conditional decisions at any point in the dialogue. If you are asking the three or four questions in succession, avoid sounding like you're reading from a checklist. When you play back the answers, try a more conversational use of the listening playback. Include the playback in the front end of the next "if you were to . . ." question. Notice how easy this is to do in the example below.

In this dialogue the customer manages a specialty foods chain. The salesperson sells telephone marketing services.

Salesperson:

If you were to go ahead with a telemarketing program, how many applications would you want at the outset?

Customer:

Probably a customer service hot line and a field sales support program.

Salesperson:

[**Plays back**] *Two applications then, a customer hot line and a program to help your outside sales people.* [**Comments**] *That will keep you in touch with a lot more clients on a regular basis.* [**Inserts a playback in the next question**] *If you were to go with the hot line and the field sales support program, when would you want to implement them?*

Customer:

There's a lot of work to be done here. We'd probably want to run a pilot in three months.

Salesperson:

[**Plays back**] *So you want a pilot by next quarter.* [**Comments**] *That allows you time to make adequate preparations. Then you'd be able to phase in the full program after a successful trial.*

Whether or not you insert a playback in the next question, the "if you were to . . ." question is easily answered. The inserted playback simply helps the rhythm of dialogue. It comes easily enough if you say it a few times. Like the other Socratic questions, these fantasy questions are drawn from the pattern of everyday speech.

THE CUSTOMER DRAWS A
CONCLUSION ABOUT YOUR ROLE

An important conclusion the customer draws is that **you had a hand in the decision-making process.** By these easily answered questions, you helped the customer think it through. The customer identifies with you and weighs alternatives in your favor, giving you an advantage over any competitor who sells virtually the same product but does not assist in this process.

The decision that counts is the customer's final decision to buy from you. If you are present when a final decision is made, chances are strong it will be in your favor. If you are not present at the final decision, the conditional decisions you facilitated have lasting influence and may carry the day for you. The customer likes the decision process you and the customer began together. Fantasy has a way of becoming reality.

SOCRATIC SKILLS NOTEBOOK

Ask easily answered questions to elicit decisions:

Lead-in	*Specific decision.*
If you were to go ahead with . . .	*when would you . . .*
	how many would you . . .
	where would you . . .
	what kind would you . . .
	and so on.

To reduce pressure, build fantasy components into the question.

- Use conditional words (*If, were to, would*).
- Exclude *I* or *we*.
- Exclude your brand name and your company name.

Support the customer's conditional decisions.

- Use brief playbacks.
- Make comments that show acceptance.

Events paint the picture of the past; decisions, the picture of the future.
Responsibility begins in seeing the future.

Chapter Eleven

Make a "No Surprises" Proposal

A SOCRATIC PROPOSAL HAS NO SURPRISES

Proposals are supposed to fit. The customer gives information that raises an expectation. The proposal should fulfill that expectation. No surprises. Surprises rattle the customer for two reasons: one, the solution is supposed to reflect what was discussed in the dialogue; and two, the customer spent valuable time in the dialogue.

If the customer has given you a perspective in response to your Socratic opener and has filled in the picture in response to your draw and access probes and easily answered questions about urgency and irritants and motivators, and if you have listened Socratically, giving full value to what you hear, there will be no surprises. Why should there be? The past has been thoroughly covered, and you understand it.

As for the customer's foray into the future to make conditional decisions, you've had a helping hand in that process, also. You've been doing your Socratic job: respecting the customer and helping the customer think and make decisions.

MAKE THE PROPOSAL FACE-TO-FACE

Now the floor is yours, and you're in perfect position to take it. The customer wanted to speak, has had the opportunity to do so, and now looks forward to hearing from you. In some businesses the salesperson makes a proposal immediately after the dialogue on needs. In others the proposal is made in a follow-up meeting. Circumstances may dictate the timing. Whatever the case, you should see to it that you deliver the proposal face-to-face.

FOLLOW A PLAN FOR DELIVERING YOUR PROPOSAL

1. Set the Stage

A face-to-face proposal needs a clear setting. Make sure the small talk and all extraneous business talk with the customer are out of the way. You want the customer to settle back into a listening mode. A statement such as "Let me summarize what you've told me" can be your signal to the customer. Because your summary represents the customer's perspective, not yours, remain seated. You are then physically closer to the source of the information you are about to review.

2. Summarize and Get Approval

Your summary is the critical part of the "no surprises" proposal for two reasons:

- Your summary is the basis for the solution you will later recommend. You capture in your summary the customer's thinking and decision making up to this point in the dialogue. Your summary takes in the entire picture: the needs, the urgency, the irritants, and the motivators that paint the past and the decisions that paint the future.
- You capture what the customer experiences as important. You thus move closer psychologically to the person seated opposite you.

Summarize the details in whatever order works best. If a time interval separates your needs interview from your proposal, you have time to review your notes and organize a presentation. Your summary should cover three categories of needs information:

1. **Facts** that describe needs or opportunities.
2. **Feelings** connected to:
   - Time urgency
   - Irritants
   - Pressure motivators
   - Success motivators
3. **Conditional decisions** made by the customer.

Quote the customer.   Search your notes for statements you can quote in the summary. Quoting the customer shows how carefully you listen. What kind of statement is quotable?

- A statement that evokes the **customer's feelings** for what is important: *"Lucia, you made a point of saying, 'Everybody on this project feels there's a lot riding on the start-up phase.' "*
- A statement about **outcomes or repercussions**: *"As you stated, Lois, 'Delay in developing a networking capacity will affect productivity.' "*
- A statement the **customer enjoyed making**: *"As you put it, Ralph, you don't want to add a wing to your museum of outmoded equipment."*

People love being quoted, but don't let quotes become a distracting device. Two or three are enough.

Include motivators when it's appropriate.   If the customer has been candid in the needs dialogue about a pressure motivator, you have to be indirect in your summary. If you were a helpful listener in the dialogue about needs, a customer might hold nothing back: "I've been pulled in by my boss. If I don't get this thing back on track, I'm finished here." Your summary should file the edge off that: "Your boss is putting a lot of pressure on you to get this back on track." The customer will know you got the message.

If your proposal is to a group of customers, the irritants and motivators are usually shared by the team; in fact, they become part of "team spirit." But a motivator communicated to you by only one party should be omitted from the summary if it is potentially embarrassing to that person.

Get the customer's approval. When you have finished your summary, ask the easily answered question:

How does that sound?

It should sound wonderful. After all it's what the customer said.

3. Make Your Recommendation an Event

Create a transition from your summary to your recommendation. Without a signal the customer doesn't see that the proposal is shifting from discussion of problem to presentation of solution. You need to ring the dinner bell. Introduce your recommendation with:

I would like to make a recommendation based on what you've told me.

Stand and use visuals to present your recommendation. Make it an event. You are taking the dialogue to a new level. Standing increases your credibility and control at the outset of the recommendation. Visuals help customers understand information that is yours, not theirs.

If some members of a buyer team are unfamiliar with your company, restate your company's credentials prior to the recommendation.

4. Pick the Right Form of Evidence

Your recommendation of products or services should be tied to benefits sought by the customer. Benefits are a promise. To increase the customer's belief the benefit will become a reality, support your recommendation with evidence.

Evidence in a sales presentation can take a variety of forms:

- References
- Statistics
- Analogy
- Endorsements
- Facts
- Exhibit
- Examples
- Expert opinion
- Demonstration

You're talking about the future, so forget about "proving" your case. You're not in court—you're not there to *verify* the past success of your product or service. You offer evidence to make it easier for the customer to step into the future. Evidence supports the buyer's risk.

To know what evidence works best, know what interests and motivates your customer.

If your product or service is truly outstanding in the market, then for different customers the same set of examples, facts, or statistics will highlight its effectiveness. Even if your company leads the field, review very carefully what you learned in the Socratic dialogue. For example, if your "why now?" questioning reveals that urgency is a factor, then an example of your solution bringing speedy results fits the customer.

Personal experience is your own first-person testimony about the benefits of your recommendation. You might think personal experience carries far less weight than an example verifiable from business or industry sources. That's not so when you have gained the customer's trust and know so much about the customer's situation that you can match it to parallel situations you've experienced. Yours is the voice of authority.

Yes, numbers crunchers consider numbers essential for credibility, but don't toss every graph at your disposal into the presentation. Every set of numbers you serve up to a numbers person is like handing a tray of white mice to Tom the Cat. A numbers person will chase those numbers around the room until every last objection has been raised and your allotment of time exhausted. Give numbers people their minimum requirement.

Soft evidence is effective, too. By contrast analogies and the opinions of experts are safe forms of evidence in that they can't be challenged. Analogies draw imaginative comparisons — for example, you might depict your product or service as a helicopter that lowers customers by rope ladder to a summit they lack the resources to scale. You thus make it easy for customers to see your product or service as effective and efficient. Analogy is soft evidence — it's only the way you think, but it can help a customer take that step into the future. Expert opinion is also merely the way somebody thinks, but some names carry a weight that tips the decision your way. Know thy customer.

Demonstrating or exhibiting your product or service is a potent way to address the customer's motivator. If user-friendliness is a customer concern, then sit the customer down and provide a user-friendly experience. Don't rush it, either. Users need to experience the friendliness. Once they feel it, you're in.

As you conclude each part of your recommendation, ask for a reaction:

How does that sound?
What's your reaction?

You have gotten agreement with your summary. Now you want agreement with your recommendation. If you get that agreement, you can close. Usually it's not that easy.

FIND THE PATH TO AGREEMENT

Customers are hesitant about a decision that leads directly to closing the business. The customer may need more information and so asks questions. The customer may also raise objections about parts of the proposal. Outright rejection, too, remains a possibility, but rejection is unlikely if the buyer is a qualified person and the dialogue has followed the Socratic principles. Closing is more likely to stick on an insurmountable objection. Handling questions, negotiating objections, and closing require Socratic procedures distinct from the proposal itself and are treated in later chapters.

The critical path of the proposal looks like this.

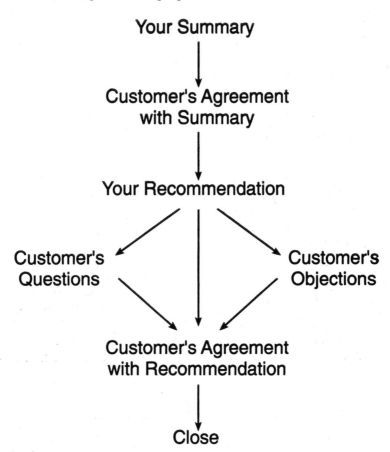

DELAY IS IN NOBODY'S INTEREST

In some businesses, the customer thinks of the proposal as a document sent by messenger or mail after the face-to-face recommendation. If you and the customer have partnered in the

Socratic process, a proposal arriving in an envelope is anticlimactic. Worse, it allows time and distance to loosen the relationship solidified by careful dialogue. If a proposal document is necessary, frame it as a *record* of your face-to-face dialogue with the customer.

The protocol of using the mail is the customer's buffer against making a decision. I recall how one salesperson who had just delivered a face-to-face proposal stood firmly by its value:

Customer:

Let's talk the week after next, Carol. In the meantime, why don't you put together a proposal?

Salesperson:

Matt, I just gave you the proposal and you agreed it was on target. Can I answer any questions about what I said?

Customer:

Well, maybe we should talk more about price.

Salesperson:

We can go over price right now.

The sale was closed during that meeting. The customer had no serious issues to be negotiated and had used up his last ploy—waiting for the proposal in the mail—to avoid making a decision. If the customer insists on a written proposal as a step on the way to agreement, then send one. But paper is no substitute for doing business face-to-face.

THE CUSTOMER REACHES THREE MORE LOGICAL CONCLUSIONS

1. The first conclusion the customer makes is that **your proposal follows from the dialogue that preceded it.** "No surprises" gives the customer a sense of continuity. The promise of the Socratic opener is realized: the customer's time was well spent. The dialogue moved along productively.

2. Another conclusion is that **your recommendation is shaped by the summary.** If you have 10 or 110 things you would

sell, you offer only what fits. If you have only one product or service to sell, you make it clear why that one offering fits. The customer feels that what you learned in the dialogue was given full value.

3. The most important conclusion the customer draws is that you are a person who can be very useful—useful not merely in bringing a solution to the case discussed, but useful in a relationship that brings together two creative sources of information. You have demonstrated an exceptional ability: You have gained access to the customer's mind and have grasped its singular perspective. Then you have applied your own knowledge—an expertise the customer does not have—to recommending a product or service that fits. Whenever the customer needs a solution, you are the type of person to rely on to make the customer's future brighter.

SOCRATIC SKILLS NOTEBOOK

Make a "no surprises" proposal. Gather momentum with a summary:

"Let me summarize what I heard you say . . ."

- Facts that describe needs or opportunities.
- Feelings connected to:
  Time urgency
  Irritants
  Pressure motivators
  Success motivators
- Conditional decisions made by the customer.

Get approval with an easily answered question:

"How does that sound?"

Make a recommendation: *"I would like to make a recommendation based on what you've told me."*

- Tie the recommendation to benefits.
- Choose evidence that fits the customer.

Ask for agreement with an easily answered question:

"What's your reaction?"

Proposals that fit are ready for agreement.

CLOSING THE SALE SOCRATICALLY

Chapter Twelve

Know the Question before You Answer

QUESTIONS MAY INTRODUCE TOPICS

When a question is used to introduce a topic, it may generate a reply that is off target. Picture a shopper in a housewares section:

- Are these kitchen knives sharp?
- Oh, yes. They have been honed with laser technology. They cut deeply, leaving no rough edge.
- Oh. My mother loves to cook but has arthritis. I'd be afraid she would get a nasty cut.

The dialogue ends awkwardly. Neither party knows what to say next. The intent of the shopper's question was not to gain information about the technology of the knives. The intent was to introduce the issue of safety. But a question like "Can we talk about the sharpness of these knives in a context of safety?" does not get asked.

Customers ask questions to clarify what the salesperson can do to help and how both customer and salesperson might work together. Many of these questions are taken at face value and given a factual answer. The customer may ask some questions, however, to express interest in a topic. Before a factual answer could be given, the topic needs to be discussed.

EVERY QUESTION HAS A PURPOSE

People frequently think in images, and the vividness of a mental image can influence the way a question is asked. The customer's question may give only part of the picture. If the salesperson picks up on the clue, the customer will fill in the rest of the picture. If the salesperson misses the clue, the dialogue bypasses a topic the customer wanted to surface.

A paper manufacturer wanted to lease a 25,000-acre tract of forest to be used for logging. The paper company's rep had an on-site meeting with the landowner. In the course of the dialogue, the landowner asked, "Is all your equipment yellow?" "Yes, yellow's the company color," the rep answered, without making anything of the question. The dialogue moved on to environmental regulations, access roads, and other topics that had to be covered in that meeting. The rep's next step was to phone in a week to make arrangements for drawing up the lease.

When the rep called back, he found the land had been leased to another company. The reason, the landowner said, was to avoid liability. The landowner kept beehives for his honeybee business on a strip of land adjacent to that being leased. Bees are attracted to yellow tractors, the landowner said. He'd heard of farm workers who had been stung. He could not risk a lawsuit.

Imagine the pang of loss felt by the rep, who expected to close on a 25,000-acre lease. "Why didn't you tell me!" the rep could only exclaim. In fact, the landowner had tried to introduce the subject of bees, but it didn't come out as "I'd like to discuss my potential liability if my bees are attracted to your equipment." The landowner's mental image was that of yellow bees around yellow tractors. Yellow was in the picture, and the question was about yellow. When the salesperson missed the signal, the customer decided to think more about the subject after the meeting.

BE THERE TO HELP THE CUSTOMER THINK

When a customer's topic does not find a way into the discussion, the salesperson is the loser. Certainly that topic will receive its due at another time. The customer may think it through alone, without help from the salesperson, or raise the subject with another party. To apply the Socratic dialogue principles—help the customer think, help the customer make decisions—you have to be there. The importance of being present when the customer is thinking and deciding is developed in connection with the customer's conditional decisions (Chapter 10). If you help the customer think conditionally about time ("If you were to go ahead . . . when would you? . . ."), as well as location, quantity, and so on, you influence those decisions.

Your advantage in dealing with topics of time, location, quantity, and others is that you know *before* the meeting that they are important. By introducing those topics yourself, you make sure you have a hand in the discussion. Other topics of importance, such as bees and liability, are known only to the customer. You will hear about bees and liability only if you help the customer think out loud. Never miss a chance to be part of the thinking.

Of course, the paper company rep offered to spray paint the equipment—you name the color, Mr. Landowner. Too late.

YOU CAN'T EXPLOIT A QUESTION YOU DON'T UNDERSTAND

A customer may be interested in a topic and asks for the salesperson's point of view. What the customer wants, however, is a genuine response, not a point of view altered to get the business.

People in the training business are frequently asked questions about the customization of training programs and materials.

Because customization can enhance training, sellers of training may assume that a customer who asks about it wants it.

Customer:

Do you customize your programs?

Salesperson:

Absolutely. We wouldn't think of giving you anything off the shelf. No two companies are the same. All our programs are created to fit the individual needs of those attending the training program. The classroom materials are developed specifically for those participants.

Customer:

Well, I'm glad you told me that because I would rather use a tried and true training program, one that has a track record with people in our industry. I wouldn't want anyone's trainers practicing on my people. Fresh approaches are great, but you can test them on somebody else.

Unlike the question about yellow equipment, this question succeeds in bringing about a vigorous discussion of the customer's topic. The salesperson helps the customer think. Unfortunately, the salesperson does so with foot stuck in mouth.

HOW CREDIBLE IS YOUR ANSWER?

You would expect the questions and answers on customization to be easy. Sellers and buyers of training know how to approach the topic with flexibility. Instead, this salesperson jumps to a conclusion and offers a response so extreme it prompts an opposite reaction from the customer. Whatever degree of need this customer might have for customization, one reason for the question is to see how the salesperson handles the topic. When a salesperson handles a topic with a sales pitch, the customer recoils. When a salesperson handles a topic by inquiring into the customer's needs, the salesperson's credibility grows.

The same dynamic occurs when you inquire about stereo equipment you don't really understand—speakers, for example. Let's say you don't know a tweeter from a woofer. When you get a high-tech sales pitch, you want to try another store. When the salesperson asks about your need and explains speakers to that level of need, you decide you've shopped enough and get out your credit card. Besides stereo speakers, you were really shopping for the right salesperson.

DON'T GO TO WAR OVER A QUESTION

In this dialogue the customer and salesperson are meeting for the first time. The customer is seeking to stock a popular line of consumer goods.

Customer:

Do you accept returns?

Salesperson:

It's not our policy. Over the years we find that if we accept returns, our customers are not committed to moving the goods. That works to our mutual disadvantage. So we've established a firm policy of working out all the arrangements beforehand. Once a customer buys, he owns the goods, not us. I'm sorry about that, but that's the way it is.

Customer:

Well, I've been stuck with an inventory of torn labels and crushed cartons. To my customers, that means damaged goods inside. There's no way I'm going through that again.

In the yellow tractor case, the salesperson missed the importance of the question. In the customization case, the salesperson guessed at the correct response to a question. Here, the customer's question is so straightforward it nudges the salesperson to say *yes* to returns. Having had experience with retailers who want to return inventory they don't move, the salesperson explains why returns are unacceptable. Each is frank with the other, and the brief discussion reaches a stalemate. That's a shame, because the customer wants the popular line of goods and the salesperson want this new business. What went wrong?

Go back to the question "Do you accept returns?" To a seller of consumer goods, the meaning seems clear: A retailer wants to buy merchandise without risk and without responsibility for moving it. But those intentions are not specified in the question. In fact, the question doesn't even specify what kind of returns and under what circumstances. As long as the question is subject to various interpretations, it is not a clear question. The salesperson bites hard on one interpretation.

Unless it is clear from the context of discussion what a question means, you must find out what it means. The Socratic approach always draws the information out of the customer:

Customer:

Do you accept returns?

Salesperson:

It's not our general policy, but *why do you ask?*

Customer:

Well, I've been stuck with an inventory of torn labels and crushed cartons. To my customers that means damaged goods inside. There's no way I'm going through that again.

Salesperson:

So you're talking about damage to the package. Should the label or carton be damaged, what we can do is . . .

Note the sequence of this dialogue:

- The customer asks a question.
- The salesperson sees that the question identifies an issue, but does not provide enough information. So the

salesperson answers briefly, in a general way, and then asks, "**Why do you ask?**"

- The customer explains in detail the topic of interest.
- The salesperson plays back in summary the customer's statements and offers a solution. If the customer's reply to "**Why do you ask**" does not clarify the issue, the salesperson would use a Socratic probe such as, "**Tell me more about the condition of these cartons your customers won't accept.**"

The brief answer is an important element. Countering one question with another can be taken as disrespect. To respect the customer, you answer to the extent you are able to answer. Because you don't understand the question, your typical answer in this situation is limited to: "Generally, yes . . ." "Generally, no . . ." or "It depends," or the verbal equivalents of these ideas. Far from being evasive, such answers are honest. Far from being shallow, these short answers respect the depth of the customer's knowledge.

DRAW OUT THE TOPIC WITH EASILY ANSWERED QUESTIONS

You give a short answer to the customer's question. You then draw out the topic by asking a question that makes it easy for the customer to speak. Once again, your Socratic approach brings ideas to light:

Why do you ask?
What are you interested in discussing?
Tell me more about . . .

You might preface the question by saying, "I'm not sure I understand your question." Some questions you just do not understand, and in a Socratic dialogue you do not guess. Do not be apologetic about seeking clarification.

RIDE A NEW TOPIC TO A CLOSE

The topic of interest introduced by a customer's question may be a mine of untouched business. In this example, the customer is a CFO responsible for the corporation's office services. The salesperson represents an outsourcing company that provides a wide variety of office services. The salesperson and customer have closed some business that reminds the CFO of a fresh topic. Lacking hands-on experience with office services, the CFO needs help in getting the topic into focus.

Customer:

Do you provide barcoding?

The question itself doesn't reveal a specific point of interest.

Salesperson:

Yes, we do, among other services . . .

"Yes, we do" is a brief, straightforward answer. The salesperson does not confuse the dialogue by explaining the many applications of barcoding and the services connected with each.

. . . Why do you ask?

The salesperson invites the customer to think out loud by probing for the point of interest.

Customer:

We need some way to track and inventory all our materials. We don't know where things are half the time.

The customer shifts from barcoding to tracking and inventory, making it clear that internal mail service is the topic of interest.

Salesperson:

So, you're having difficulty lo-
cating the things you need.
**Tell me more about tracking
and inventory.**

The salesperson plays back
for understanding and follows with a Socratic probe.

Customer:

Sometimes the mail gets from
one office to another in a day—
sometimes in a week. We don't
get faxes and priority docu-
ments right away. It's a mess.
We need to locate correspon-
dence quickly.

Now the customer adds ur-
gency and critical detail.
But for the probes, the irritant may not have surfaced.
The topic of interest has
now evolved into a fully expressed need.

Salesperson:

So you want your employees to
receive information promptly,
and that requires a system for
tracking and inventory of mail.

The salesperson summa-
rizes to elicit the customer's
agreement.

Customer:

Yes.

This new piece of business
can close right now.

THE CUSTOMER DRAWS A
CONCLUSION FROM YOUR ANSWERS

Helping the customer surface a topic for discussion helps the customer think. Not every issue important to the customer is thoroughly worked out in the customer's mind. Consequently,
customers may ask misleading questions. By getting to the real
issue, you advance the dialogue. **The customer sees you as
someone who has a nose for what is important.** In one more
way your stature grows, and the relationship between you and the
customer is strengthened.

The topic the customer wants to introduce may be the one last thing kicking around in the customer's mind. Once it's out on the table, the customer experiences satisfaction with the dialogue, and the sale could close on the wave of that satisfaction. If you have helped the customer access that "one last thing," the customer will accept your help in making the final decision.

SOCRATIC SKILLS NOTEBOOK

The customer's question may introduce a topic of interest. Draw out the customer's interest before attempting to answer in detail.

1. Give a brief, general answer to the question.
2. Use an easily answered question to draw out more detail:
   - *"Why do you ask?"*
   - *"What are you interested in discussing?"*
   - *"Tell me more about . . ."*

Never miss a topic the customer wants to introduce.
Never miss a chance to help the customer think.

Chapter Thirteen

Go behind the Objection

OBJECTIONS ARE THE LION'S ROAR

The lion roars, reminding you just how much is at stake. By voicing an objection, the customer lets you know that making a commitment is a risk. Impressive as your proposal has been, it's only a promise of a better future. The customer has to make the commitment before you deliver on the promise. If anything in the proposal seems amiss, the customer will test you on that point of perceived risk.

OBJECTIONS ARE A SIGN OF INTEREST

An objection is not a rejection. Your "no surprises" proposal has demonstrated your professionalism in summarizing the dialogue between you. In that proposal the customer saw your product or service appealingly presented. Quite possibly, the objection is nothing more than a request for information. Beyond information, the objection may be a demand that one or more terms of the proposal be changed. Broadly speaking, the terms of a proposal that frequently draw objections are:

- The *price* of the solution you offer.
- The *timing* you specified in the proposal.
- The *quality* of the solution—for example, the customer wants you to commit more time or personnel for the solution to be applied at a higher level of performance.
- The *fitness* of a part of the solution: "This part isn't right for us," or "We don't need that item," says the customer.
- The *follow-up*, or servicing of the deal.

You could list more categories or squeeze others into these five. Remember that any objection, no matter what category, may be either a request for information or a demand for change.

CHECK YOUR MINDSET ON OBJECTIONS

You should know as you enter into any sales dialogue that you will probably have objections. Will you cringe when the lion roars? Examine your strength on this point beforehand. How confident are you that your proposal can bring a solution, can bring progress to the customer's world? How enthusiastic are you about the product or service? If the customer doesn't buy, you would be disappointed in losing the business. Would you also feel the customer made an error in not choosing the best?

Not everything about your company and its products or services can be perfect. But your level of comfort with the solutions your company develops for customers has to sustain you when the customer raises objections.

Price is perhaps the most common objection, and many salespeople are not authorized to be flexible with price. If your discomfort with the price of your product or service outweighs *your* perception of its value, your mindset will burden you in handling objections. Salespeople need to talk to someone about that kind of discomfort. Sales managers may have helpful advice. Often, the person who can help most is a colleague with a positive outlook, a fellow salesperson who feels the solution is worth the cost to the customer. When a colleague's confidence in your company's solutions has generated a solid sales record, you have a role model.

YOU DON'T UNDERSTAND THE OBJECTION

Veteran salespeople will say they've heard every objection, and they probably have. But the next time a common objection is raised, the veteran salesperson won't know what it means. "You're too expensive" is certainly a common objection. Isn't "too expensive" clear? No, it's not. Too expensive to pay in one installment? Too expensive to pay right now? Too expensive in relation to *what?*

When you don't know what the other person is talking about, you aren't going to know what *you're* talking about. When you don't know what you're talking *about*, it's easy to become defensive and begin talking *against:*

Customer:

The PCs are just too expensive for our company.

Salesperson:

Too expensive? They're really not, when you consider those PCs can be positioned any way you want, for direct feed to video or an LCD panel or . . .

Customer:

I still think you charge too much.

Salesperson:

Remember, you get a round-the-clock service package. The benefits to you are we're on call 24 hours a day.

This dialogue will go nowhere. Regardless of the features or benefits restated, the objection will block the sale. The customer is thinking: *"I said it twice and she didn't hear me! I don't care how many benefits she cites. It's just too expensive!"*

GET RID OF YOUR ASSUMPTIONS

Aren't some objections obvious? Don't bet on it. Take the example of the auto dealer who has a customer in the showroom ready to buy but meets an objection about the seat covering.

Customer:

That beige is ugly.

The salesperson's heart sinks. The seats of this model come in beige or blue. Blue seats the salesperson would have to "locate" with another dealer. Getting a car from another dealer cuts profitability. The salesperson starts to say, "But everybody likes beige!" bites his tongue, and asks, **"Why do you say that?"**

Is this a dumb question? That beige is ugly means that beige is ugly. What's hard to understand about a four-word sentence? Everything, if the word *ugly* doesn't refer to the word *beige*.

Customer:

That beige is ugly.

Salesperson:

Ugly—*why do you say that?*

Customer:

Because that velour fabric won't hold up. With the use I give a car, it'll get worn in a few months and look ugly.

Salesperson:

So the fabric is the problem. If beige is okay with you, I have the seat in leather. Feels great and lasts. Have it right outside.

Customer:

You do?

Salesperson:

Let's walk over to the lot and have you sit behind the wheel.

Do people say *beige* when they mean *velour*? People say what they see. The customer was looking at an undesirable fabric that happened to be beige. A fabric that's wrong in a car that's right creates pressure on the customer. The customer relieves the pressure by expressing resistance in a handful of words. Whatever words come out, the customer uses. To the customer the words don't matter; expressing resistance is what matters. It's your job to find the meaning. You can't deal with *ugly* if you think color is the objection.

In a Socratic dialogue, you give full value to what the customer says. Giving full value means you understand the customer's statement and respond accordingly. But you can't attribute full value if you don't know what the customer means. Do you know what the customer means when the customer hasn't clarified the meaning? Only if you're a mindreader. Just as the wording of a question can disguise an issue the customer wants to introduce, the wording of an objection can disguise its meaning.

For the Socratic process to work, the first thing you must get rid of is your assumption that you understand the objection.

Assumptions are necessary time-savers. You couldn't get through a workday if you had to examine everything. Every trade and every profession allows certain assumptions to be made. Every trade and every profession also has red-flag moments—moments to stop and look more closely. In expressing an objection, the customer is revealing a perceived risk—perceived danger for the one who makes the sale happen! For the salesperson, that's a red-flag moment.

MAKE THE OBJECTION SPECIFIC

Most objections are stated in general terms. "Too expensive" is general. To make the objection specific, use a Socratic approach. Go behind the objection. Draw the truth out of the other party. Have the customer break the objection into its parts.
The Socratic procedure goes like this:

- Play back the objection in a few words. You may echo the key word. Let the prospect know that you heard.

- Make the objection specific. After playing back the objection, ask, **"Why do you say that?"** or **"Please tell me exactly what that means."** Unless you know exactly what the objection is, you can't answer it.

Customer:
You're too expensive.
Salesperson:
[Plays back] *You find us too expensive.* [Probes] *Why do you say that?*
Customer:
Your competition is 10 percent cheaper.

Now the salesperson knows the specific meaning of *"You're too expensive."* In other dialogues with other customers, "you're too expensive" could mean:

- *"Figure in maintenance costs and repairs excluded from warranty and your quote puts us over budget."*
- *"Our cash flow won't permit a lump-sum payment."*
- *"Well, add to your price our cost of hiring someone to operate the equipment and it takes us too high."*

Each of these answers reveals a different reason for the objection *"You're too expensive."* To each of the above specific objections, the salesperson could negotiate a different solution. By failing to pursue the specific point of the objection, the salesperson won't have the information needed to help the customer work through the objection.

FIND THE CUSTOMER'S CONCERN

In going behind the objection, don't stop at the specific meaning of the statement. Find out why the customer raises the objection. What leads the customer to make the objection? If you understand the concerns, you are better prepared to negotiate with the customer over the objection.

Customer:

This deal is too expensive for us.

Salesperson:

Too expensive. Why do you say that?

Customer:

The most we're willing to pay for the equipment is $83,000.

Salesperson:

That's $12,000 below the price quoted. *How did you arrive at that figure?*

Customer:

We have to be sure we can repair equipment during the first year, when use is the heaviest. In the past year we had costs of a thousand a month not covered by the warranty.

Now the salesperson sees the picture. The specific meaning of "too expensive" is the $12,000 above the $83,000 the customer wants to pay. The concern for that $12,000 figure is derived from experience with repair costs. With this knowledge the salesperson may be able to negotiate an agreement on price, perhaps by changing some service options in the original proposal or by taking another approach.

ASK EASILY ANSWERED QUESTIONS ABOUT THE OBJECTION

Two Socratic principles are in play: You are helping the customer think so you can help the customer make decisions. Your request for clarification should be as simple as possible. These questions can be selected to fit the context of the dialogue and may be used in conjunction with each other:

> *Please tell me exactly what you mean.*
> *Why do you say that?*
> *How did you arrive at that?*

The customer's answers to these Socratic questions are critically important. True to the classic Socratic dialogue, the answers may provide the key to unlocking the objection and negotiating a go-ahead to the close. Let the customer know you know the importance of the concern: "Let's go over what you said, so that nothing gets left behind."

So that nothing does get left behind, make sure your playbacks capture the key facts *and* the person.

THE CUSTOMER DRAWS A LOGICAL CONCLUSION ABOUT YOU

You certainly are different! Instead of refuting the objection, you played it back and asked questions to better understand it. You showed interest in the issue or concern behind the objection. You're not like salespeople who argue and bully or try to bury the objection in a snowstorm of data. Following the objection, it takes only a few minutes of dialogue for the customer to reach this conclusion.

Once the customer perceives you as a person who will listen to an objection and learn about it, the issue itself looks different. The point in your proposal that the customer objects to is still there and so is the objection. **But negotiating with you is less risky. You are committed to understanding the customer.**

SOCRATIC SKILLS NOTEBOOK

You don't understand the objection you hear. To handle it Socratically, go behind the objection.

1. Make the objection specific.
2. Probe for the concern behind the objection.
   - Play back the objection in a word or two.
   - Ask easily answered questions.
     "Please tell me exactly what you mean."
     "Why do you say that?"
     "How did you arrive at that?"

When you don't know what the customer is talking about, you don't know what you're talking about.

Chapter Fourteen

Get Ready to Negotiate Objections

YOU CAN'T JUST REACT

Many salespeople simply react to an objection. A reaction is a first or "gut" response; it establishes a beginning. Reactions don't give you a plan to proceed; they don't even have a goal. After reacting to the customer's objection, you can end up "winging it" the rest of the way.

If you simply react to an objection, you may concede what you shouldn't. With a customer who has done business with you for years, you may lean too heavily on your enjoyment of the relationship. If the customer is new, you may try too hard to please. You can become a victim of your enthusiasm for the sale.

The reaction on the other end is inflexibility: Try to argue down the objection. Crawl into a concrete bunker, citing company policy. Nobody can score a hit on you in the bunker, but that doesn't help the relationship.

KNOW WHERE YOU STAND

A customer is asking you to change a part of the deal you proposed. You feel you've done your best: you've asked questions that helped the customer think, you've given full value to the customer's story in your Socratic listening, you've earned agreement with your summary, and you've matched a recommendation to the picture you see. But you can't move toward a close. There's this hitch.

Before you negotiate your go-ahead to the close, you have a few pre-negotiation tasks. Preparation to negotiate takes place at two levels:

1. Review your pre-negotiation outlook. Look for the landmarks that tell you where you are. When I was a pilot, I found lakes made the terrain distinctive. Check your view of the entire sales process. Pay attention to the factors that help you get your bearings.
   - Your goals.
   - The customer's goals.
   - Your value to the customer.
2. Review your pre-negotiation strategy.
   - Know all the objections.
   - Know what they mean and the concerns behind them.

CHECK YOUR GOALS

Do an awareness check. Who are you as a salesperson, and what do you want and need? You don't have to check over your professional status every time you hear an objection. You do have to be aware of it as you go on a sales call.

Checkpoint 1: Your sales revenue is one measure of your performance. You want to negotiate in a way that supports your sales number in the long run. Trying to hold to price will support your numbers; knee-jerk discounting will not.

Checkpoint 2: You also want to partner with this customer. Confrontations do not build relationships. Socratic dialogue does.

Checkpoint 3: You have an account list. In partnering with this customer, you have to play fair. You shouldn't sell a product or service differently to every customer—if for no other reason than that word gets around. Ask yourself, "Whatever I do with this objection from this customer, would I do it with another customer?"

CHECK THE CUSTOMER'S GOALS

As part of a cost-cutting strategy, corporate management may pressure buyers to find less-expensive solutions. Some buyers respond by trying to intimidate the salesperson. After a few battle lines have been drawn on price, the salesperson tends to believe price is the only issue. That's true when price exceeds the budget. That's also true when competition directs the customer's attention away from value received by focusing only on price paid. In a price war the downward slide of prices usually results in the customer not only paying less, but getting less.

PLAN TO HOLD PRICE AND INCREASE VALUE GIVEN

Customers want value for what they pay. When the customer objects to price, what are your first thoughts? Price objections routinely trigger this response: Can I lower the price, should I lower the price, and how much should I lower the price? Instead of routinely going into the discount mode of negotiating, try holding the price and increasing the value the customer will receive. Adding value doesn't necessarily increase costs. By now, you know what's important to the customer. You may be able to enhance the deal for the customer at no cost or at a cost that doesn't negate the advantage of getting your price.

Getting your price by adding value cements the relationship. Both customer and salesperson sense they have gained something important through an honest interaction.

YOUR PROFITABILITY HELPS THE CUSTOMER

The profitability of your company is to the advantage of the customer. To partner with the customer long term, your company needs to apply profits to grow and become the best. Price directly affects profitability. As a wise old sales manager put it, "Don't look for customers who will pay less and get less. Look for customers who will pay more and get more. Keep everybody happy."

Keeping everybody happy requires mutual recognition of needs. You build trust and ultimately a salesperson-customer relationship by recognizing many customer needs. Fundamentally, your Socratic approach recognizes the customer's need to be heard and to have an impact on the dialogue. In the course of the Socratic dialogue, you recognize the business needs the customer discusses and their impact on the customer's organization. From there you go on to recognize the impact of those needs on this individual customer—how it all affects the customer, from the meanest irritant to the noblest ambition the customer has for success.

It remains for the customer to recognize your needs. You are not an anonymous order-taker or a take-a-number vendor queuing up for an isolated transaction. Socratically, you are there to be an ongoing resource for the customer. To be that, your sales revenue needs to support your company's profits so that, in turn, your company can afford to make available to the customer salespeople as good as you are. The customer needs to see doing business with you as an investment.

KNOW YOUR VALUE TO THE CUSTOMER

You are a valuable resource. By taking a Socratic approach to the sales dialogue, you have led the customer to draw conclusions about you personally. You are systematic, alert, and reliable. You make the time productive. The customer thinks more clearly when you're there. You are worthy of trust. Never underestimate the impression you make upon the customer in a Socratic dialogue.

The customer has invested time in you—if not months or years, at least the time of a meeting. Remember, the clock runs on the customer. By the time you reach the postproposal negotiation stage, the customer can ill afford to start over with somebody else. The customer's options are with competing proposals, each of which has something objectionable about it.

You also bring a valuable product or service. Your "no surprises" proposal positioned it strategically. Your stand-up, face-to-face delivery made the proposal an event. None of that is lost on your customer. Whatever objection is holding up the decision to buy, the customer values what you sell. Objections are a way of expressing a desire to buy.

DON'T GIVE AWAY WHAT YOU CAN TRADE FOR

When you hear the first objection, you may sense that you're just this little bit away from closing. You may feel you'd just like to give in, give this issue away, and go on to the next customer. After all, you've worked hard. Better to go home with something rather than nothing.

Let's say you represent a firm that sets up corporate benefits plans. Your customer—called a client in your business—is a benefits manager named Alice. (Alice appeared in the dialogue on page 55, where she answered the question, "What makes it urgent?") You've made a proposal. This client's first objection is to your proposed 90-day assessment of the needs of the client's employees. "Still too much time," Alice says. You agree to 60 days. Chopping four weeks off the assessment project means putting extra researchers on the team. You're not sure exactly what that costs you. Of course, the client is paying for the project and sees researchers as your problem. Well, you think, I'm landing a big fish here . . . You say, "Okay."

Then Alice objects that your proposal assigns only one person as ongoing benefits consultant to the office of the benefits manager. You probe for the specific meaning of this second objection. Alice says consultants change jobs and she doesn't want to start over with a new face. She wants a back-up consultant assigned to the account. Well, you think, working out a back-up arrangement is an administrative problem. Of course, the client will pay for only one consultant, but on the other hand, the client isn't really using the back-up consultant. As you say *yes*, you begin figuring how you'll work it out back home. You notice you have a headache.

Now it's Client 2, Salesperson 0, but you can smell ink on the contract. But wait—Alice wants "more paper" for the employees. You probe for the specific meaning of this third objection. Ah, yes, a blizzard of bulletins and reports generated by your company for reading by the employees. And the benefit manager's underlying concern? To assure every employee that the experts have not come and gone; no, they watch over the benefits plan every day.

You had proposed a quarterly bulletin. The client wants a lot more paper. You consider computer time, document editing, production, and mailing. No, you cannot. Management would shoot you. You cannot say *yes* one more time.

DON'T GET STUCK WITH WHAT YOU CAN'T GIVE

You're in trouble. You can't go back to the beginning and try to bundle all these issues into a better deal for yourself. You already conceded to the first two objections. You gave those issues away. They're gone. The client has them in her knapsack.

You're stuck with what you can't give. So you say *no* to the third objection. Now the client has three options:

1. Buy from somebody else. You lose.
2. Postpone a decision and shop around, in the meantime leaving you hanging. You don't lose, but you hurt.

3. Grumble a bit and finally do the deal with you, with the first two concessions included. You win, but you still lose.

This last option gives you the business. Even so, your original proposal has been changed by the client. You get nothing in return.

KNOW ALL THE OBJECTIONS BEFORE NEGOTIATING

Your mistake was to begin the negotiation too soon—without all the key facts. One critical fact is the *number* of separate issues around which the customer has an objection. Is there one objection? Big or small, a single objection is easier to negotiate. Six objections? Multiple objections may be the result of new developments in the customer's needs picture. Or the result of an intervention by the customer's boss or other parties. Both cases leave you to deal with factors that may not have been dealt with in the Socratic dialogue.

After making the first objection specific and learning the concern behind it, find out if there are other objections and what they are. To help the customer think, you need an easily answered question.

ASK AN EASILY ANSWERED "SUPPOSE QUESTION"

This easily answered question embodies the strategy to defer any negotiation of the first objection until all the issues are on the table. Your question then should remove the first issue or objection from the discussion—parking it temporarily to the side—and then surface any remaining issues. To achieve this, you need to formulate the question with each idea carefully stated. Indeed, every word in this "suppose question" has a purpose:

> *Suppose we were able to resolve that issue.*
> *I know it's not resolved right now, but just suppose we could.*
> *Are there any other issues standing in the way of our doing business?*

The "suppose" question is easy for the customer to answer. Either the objection first stated will stand alone or it will be joined to other issues. And the customer has every reason to be candid because it's in the customer's interest to express objections.

Two sentences precede the actual question about other issues: (1) *"Suppose we were able to resolve that issue."* (2) *"I know it's not resolved right now, but just suppose we could."* This conditional lead-in to the question is absolutely necessary! Only when the first objection has been put on a shelf can you ask, "Are there any other issues? . . ." The "suppose" lead-in shows respect for the customer. The lead-in lets the customer know that the first objection will be addressed and have its place in the dialogue. The "suppose" lead-in also helps the customer think—by separating one objection from others that need to discussed.

It's a good idea to rehearse the "Suppose . . ." question. Like the Socratic opener, the suppose question is a composite of several key ideas. Because the suppose question is longer than the other easily answered questions you use in Socratic selling, it requires practice. The purpose of rehearsing words is that they become readily available when you need them. Invest your energy in thinking about your dialogue, not in formulating words. If you try to find the words each time, you'll find that your stumbling distracts you—and the customer—from the suppose question.

Rehearsal removes obstacles. It's easier for the customer to understand when you know what to say; harder for the customer when you are groping for words. When you can ask the "Suppose . . ." question smoothly, you help the customer think.

THE CUSTOMER REACHES A LOGICAL CONCLUSION

If the customer says there are no other objections, the customer must conclude that only one issue is—in your carefully chosen words—"standing in the way." **An objection that stands alone is diminished because it is alone.** It's the *only* thing. Even the customer must look upon it that way.

If there are other issues, then you will reach for an understanding of each. The customer, as part of the Socratic approach, becomes involved in helping you understand. Perhaps the customer also arrives at a better understanding. At the very least the customer concludes that you have listened Socratically, have given full value to the objections, and are now prepared to negotiate.

SOCRATIC SKILLS NOTEBOOK

Know your value to the customer.

- You are a reliable resource.
- The customer has invested time in you.
- You offer a valuable product or service.

Know all the objections before negotiating.

- Don't give away what you can trade for.
- Don't get stuck with what you can't give.

Ask an easily answered "suppose question":

"Suppose we were able to resolve this issue. I know it's not re-solved right now, but just suppose we could. Are there any other issues standing in the way of our doing business?"

Never underestimate the impression you make upon the customer in a Socratic dialogue.

Chapter Fifteen

Negotiate the Get-Give Way

THE CUSTOMER WANTS CHANGES

You proposed a deal. You made a recommendation of a product or service and included the terms of the deal and price, most likely, and many of the conditional decisions about timing and other factors that you and the customer had discussed. The customer wants the solution you recommend, but . . .

You've worked with the "but . . .": You have asked questions that get to the specific meaning of the first objection. You have asked questions that get to the customer's concern behind the first objection. You've done this for each objection, so you know how many there are and what they are before attempting to negotiate.

Now, how are you going to handle the demand for changes? The changes are, in effect, amendments to your proposal. The amendments add up to something more for the customer and something less for you. For many salespeople, the only question is "*How much* less will they have to accept in order to get the business?"

CONCESSIONS HURT THE RELATIONSHIP

If you immediately concede, what does that say about the integrity of the proposal? If, for example, the objection is price and you immediately cut the price, your action suggests that the original price was inflated. Of course, some objections are minor; you can easily concede a point of no importance. Other objections merely require that you substitute terms of equal value, so you would be conceding nothing. But a substantial objection can't be conceded without the customer at some point wondering how many other crossbeams in your proposal might collapse if shaken. The customer may begin to question the confidence you've earned. Concessions don't help you work together.

TRADE; DON'T CONCEDE

Instead of negotiating to get less, trade. Trading is an expanded form of selling. Trading introduces variety and flexibility into the exchange of values between salesperson and customer. In the narrowest form of selling, a single item desired by a customer is purchased for a fixed price. There's little or no space to maneuver. The customer either buys or doesn't. A customer who wants the item badly may experience a conflict over price and voice an objection. Such objections are expressions of complaints rather than continued interest and usually signal the customer's walk-away from the transaction. The narrower the deal, the more vulnerable it is to such objections.

Trading sees the potential sale as a successful event in the ongoing relationship between customer and salesperson. Trading encourages continued interest on the customer's part, despite one or more objections. The emphasis shifts from an exchange of the salesperson's *what* for the customer's *what* to a search for gains and benefits. Gains and benefits do not have to be at the other party's expense. Gains and benefits are facets of a solution broad enough and flexible enough to be seen from many sides.

EXPAND THE OPTIONS

To trade, increase the number of issues under discussion. Each issue can generate terms of the deal that provide a value for you, for the customer, or both. You increase the number of gains and benefits in the deal. As the terms are changed, the total value of the deal to each party changes.

The change in total value doesn't mean more value for one and less for the other. You are trading for gains and benefits that are weighted individually and subjectively: Your one orange for somebody's two apples doesn't get you a basket of fruit better than the other person's. It gets you a basket you want.

The more options you create, the more latitude you have to work out an agreement satisfactory to you and the customer.

The options carry you beyond the dimension of the customer's demand for a certain number of changes. The expanded options are Socratic: The customer has more to think about and more to decide upon.

YOU LIKE WINNING, SO MAKE A "GET" LIST

You want to feel good about yourself as a salesperson, so why not get something you didn't ask for in the original proposal? Remember, *get* does not mean get the business. Typically, salespeople think only of the *get* as the sale itself. This *get* upgrades the value of the sale to you and your company.

The "get" list is the hardest. The "gets" are optional ways of doing the deal that are in your favor. To be sure, the customer isn't going to help you with the list. The customer has reshaped your proposal with a framework of demands. To break out of that framework, you have to think of getting before giving. Think of getting independently of giving.

One way to make a list of gets is to review the conditional decisions the customer made during the dialogue about needs. You included these conditional decisions about when and how and where the business should be conducted in the summary of your proposal. The customer approved your summary. Why shouldn't the customer have approved? These conditional decisions were exactly what the customer wanted! Now it's time to consider how these decisions can be modified to give you what you want:

1. **When.** By changing the timing, can you rearrange the terms of the deal to provide yourself with a benefit? Some examples might be more lead time for you to deliver the product or service, payment up front, or acceleration of payments.

2. **Who.** Access to other people and departments within the buyer's corporation is valuable to you. Referrals, letters of introduction, or endorsements can generate gains in your other sales efforts. "Would you call so-and-so?" Such access goes outside the frame of reference established by the sale.

3. **What kind.** Perhaps the products or services described in the proposal can be restructured to your advantage without removing the benefits the customer wants. Take a look at the way you administrate the deal. Is it possible to simplify your company's administrative burden and so increase profitability?

4. **How many/How much.** Can the deal be expanded to involve more participants on the customer side? Will they purchase ancillary products or services from you? Can the contract be extended?

5. **Where.** Location: Their place or yours, whichever is better for you. If you have to spend a week doing business on the Amazon River, can they get you an air-conditioned raft? (There are such things!)

THE CUSTOMER LIKES WINNING, SO MAKE A "GIVE" LIST

The "give" list isn't hard to get started. The customer has already given you a few ideas in the objections and demands for changes. Of course, the customer would put all the desired changes on your "give-to-customer" list: reduce the price, upgrade the quality, accelerate delivery, increase service, and so on.

You may put one or more of the changes the customer wants on your give list. Once on your give list, these changes are no longer concessions. You are trading with these items of value for items on your get list. Can you see the wisdom of completing a get list first?

The criterion for your contribution to the give list must be value to the customer. Once again, listening pays dividends. Think back to the customer's answers to your probes early in the dialogue: about what is important to the customer; about the impact of urgency, irritants, or motivators. Think back to the customer's conditional decisions and the brief conversation following each decision in which you supported the decision. How else can you find a benefit for the customer in what kind, when, where, and so on?

In finding ways for the customer to gain from the deal, you're saying, in effect, "We're close to an agreement. What would you say if you had (such and such)? . . ." In addition to finding fresh values, make sure you have highlighted benefits already in the deal as originally proposed. Don't assume the customer understands every facet of the deal that is immediately or potentially beneficial. Look for points you may have taken for granted. Show the customer how gains can be made: "I'd like to call attention to something that you can develop to great advantage . . ."

RE-USE YOUR GET LIST

You don't have to start with a blank sheet every time you negotiate with a get-give list. Be on the lookout for the same three or four gets. You already know their value to you and your company. The same gets can be negotiated with customers in different industries. Access to other potential buyers in the customer's organization is a potential get in many businesses. Experience will teach you the feasibility of each get. Gaining more lead time, for example, may be possible in some cases and not in others.

KNOW YOUR STOPPING POINT

Every get-give list has a stopping point. You stop because to give any more would be a bad deal. Not all business is good business. What tells you to stop? Go back to the criteria for supporting your company's interests.You may have to stop if the customer wants a deal that requires higher maintenance and lower revenue. You may have to stop to safeguard quality. As the saying goes, everybody wants it fast, cheap, and good, but the most anybody can get is two of the three. Nothing can hurt you more than cutting back on good.

Stopping points more frequently come into play when the negotiation is about one issue, for example, price. When you have expanded the options, the stopping point can be avoided through trading gets and gives.

SAY NO SOCRATICALLY

A customer may make one or more demands that you cannot meet. The demands leave the proposed deal unbalanced. It's not a way you want to do business. In that case:

- Play back what the customer wants! "Alice, let me be sure I'm clear on what you want."
- Include the customer's interest or concern: "Bear with me while I try to put this into your perspective . . ."
- Decline the demand by introducing an explanation: **"I want you to know why that's further than I can go."**

The "I want you to know . . ." statement is a Socratic way of saying *no.* Explaining why you stop respects the customer and helps the customer think. And it obliges you to have a compelling reason for saying *no.* Remember who the customer is. You're saying *no* to the lion.

LET YOUR "WHY NOT" EDUCATE THE CUSTOMER

Developing a "No, and here's why" statement matters. Your explanation can make it possible for the customer to walk your way. In a Socratic dialogue each party learns from the information the other brings to the table. Each party gives full value to that information, which means understanding it and according it a place in the dialogue. The customer needs to know your thinking on the obstacle that now stands in your way. The influence of your explanation—with other factors—can lead to agreement.

The best explanation is one that centers on the customer's interests and the benefits the customer stands to lose or gain. By playing back the customer's desired change and the interest or concern behind the change, you begin with the customer interests in focus.

It may be that the changes the customer wants do not improve the deal for the customer. If so, educate the customer. Show how a particular customer benefit might be lost in the change or how the change may work against the customer's own interest. Customers are often short-sighted. They want some immediate advantage that weakens the solution you have proposed.

Prepare the way for a counteroffer that enhances the benefits you had originally proposed or introduces new benefits. Support your lost benefits/gained benefits explanation with evidence. Evidence educates. You can use your personal experience with similar deals; you can cite industry examples; you can go to your database for whatever is relevant; you can quote those who know the business.

In explaining why you must decline the customer's changes, you are saying you'd hate to see the customer miss out on benefits. You are also slowing down the negotiation process. The customer needs time to think.

TO KEEP NEGOTIATING, ASK AN EASILY ANSWERED QUESTION

However respectfully you decline the customer's demand, you are refusing to take a step the customer wanted. The negotiation is at a sensitive juncture. Fortunately, you've been thinking and you have a counteroffer. Make it easy for the customer to say *yes* to discussing it.

Would you like to discuss what I think might work?

Remember, the customer wants a solution, and each counteroffer is another proposed solution. Invite the customer to join you in talking about your counteroffer!

MAKE A "GET-GIVE" COUNTEROFFER

The get-give counteroffer follows the "If you . . . , then I . . ." formula.

- The counteroffer lays down a condition beginning with the words "If you . . ." The condition is the customer's commitment to one or more of the gets from your get list. Which of the gets you choose depends, of course, on the situation. The condition is expressed by the introductory word *if*.

- The counteroffer finishes with a commitment on your part to deliver one or more of the gives on your give list. Again, what you choose to give depends on the situation. Your commitment is expressed by the words "then I will . . ."

JOT ALL THE PIECES ON PAPER

Think back to the case of Alice, the benefits manager, in Chapter 14. Alice got a few concessions from a salesperson who wasn't prepared to negotiate. The salesperson, a benefits consultant, failed to use a suppose question to uncover all the objections. By failing to set up the negotiation skillfully, the salesperson was not in a position to continue.

To see how a skillful negotiation might play out, put yourself in that salesperson's shoes one more time. You know what Alice wants and why, and what you want and why.

You sit down with a pencil and pad to write out a deal:

Client's demand for changes in my proposal

1. Reduce the research project from 90 to 60 days.
   - Client's concern: Needs it sooner. (Alice is caught in time urgency and has a pressure motivator—senior management.)
   - Downside for me: We pay the cost of accelerated schedule.

2. Assign a back-up consultant to the benefits manager's office.
   - Client's concern: A buffer against consultant turnover.
   - Downside: An administrative headache, sure to draw fire.

3. A monthly report to client company employees.
   - Client's concern: Reassures the employees. (The benefits manager's success motivator is to get the employees more than they expect in terms of expert supervision.)
   - Downside: Data overkill, costly to administrate.

My "get" list

1. An introduction to their pension manager and risk manager.
2. I present the completed project to their senior management.
3. A shot at outsource management of an ongoing service such as records keeping.

4. Performance-based increase in the project fee if it's completed in 50 days or less.

My "give" list

1. We absorb the cost of compressing the research to 60 days.
   • My reason: Critical to the client.
2. Assign a senior consultant to the benefits manager's office.
   • My reason: Avoids a back-up consultant arrangement. Seniority provides the client with stability—a client concern.
3. Along with the quarterly report in the original proposal, we supply speakers for a quarterly "benefits forum."
   • My reason: The client values the exposure, and a forum is neither costly nor burdensome for us.

DECLINE, EXPLAIN WHY, AND MAKE A COUNTEROFFER

Salesperson:

Alice, you've asked for 60 days, a back-up consultant to the office of benefits manager, and a monthly report for your employees. Your reasons for these changes we've already discussed. Let me summarize them: You can't wait 90 days, you can't risk losing the consultant and starting over with a new person, and your employees need more assurance that their benefits are receiving attention.

Customer:

That's right.

Salesperson:

Let me explain why your changes—taken together—take me further than I can go. Two of your changes, the 60 days and the monthly report, increase our costs. With our costs being increased in two ways, it's difficult for me to give you a solution that works as you want it to. My experience tells me it's better to funnel our costs into the 60 days, which pays off for you up front. As for the monthly report, it loses its charm after a few months. Also, the back-up consultant and the monthly report create an administrative burden. Alice, you know that what's a burden for any administration, yours or ours, will break down eventually. You would be left without a service you expected to have. We need a process that works consistently for you.

Customer:

Look, I know you have responsibilities to your company. I have a job to do here, too—that's why you've got to change your proposal.

Salesperson:

Alice, would you like to discuss what I think might work?

Customer:

Sure, as long as I get what I need for this project to work.

Salesperson:

Alice, if you can help me out in four areas, I will give you what you need for the project to work. Most of the help I want is outside this project: (1) I'd like an introduction to your pension manager and risk manager. (2) I'd like to present the completed project to your senior management. (3) Get me a shot at one of your ongoing services, such as records keeping . . .

Customer:

I can't wait to hear the last one.

Salesperson:

A performance-based increase in the project fee if it's completed in 50 days or less.

Customer:

You're dreaming.

Salesperson:

Hold on, Alice; there's more to my offer. **If—I say, if—you can help me with those four, I'll give you:** (1) the project in 60 days, all costs absorbed by us; (2) a senior consultant, eight years with our company. This is a much better value for you, because you get not only stability but greater experience and expertise; (3) to support the quarterly report, a quarterly forum where our consultant does Q&A and the whole expert bit face-to-face with your employees.

Customer:

I like that forum idea. But no monthly report?

Salesperson:

Quarterly report. And a quarterly forum. You could call it "The Benefits Manager's Forum."

Customer:

Now I like it even better. I'm willing to do the introductions and referrals you want, but you've got to realize senior management might stiff us on your presentation. I don't mind paying the 50-day fee if I can get it that fast.

Salesperson:

We'll try. You know you've got it in 60 for sure at no added fee.

Customer:

We have a deal.

THE CUSTOMER DRAWS A CONCLUSION ABOUT SOCRATIC NEGOTIATING

The customer concludes that you have struck a productive deal. Besides a deal, you have strengthened the relationship by negotiating changes with mutual respect. If you can negotiate, the rest is easy. You and the customer can disagree, can communicate well while disagreeing, can have both players win. **It adds up to this: You make a good business partner.**

SOCRATIC SKILLS NOTEBOOK

The customer wants changes. Start by expanding the options.

- Make a get list.
- Make a give list.

Decline and explain.

Decline the changes that take you beyond your stopping point. Explain your rationale for stopping: *"Let me explain why that's further than I can go."*

Ask an easily answered question to introduce a counteroffer:

"Would you like to discuss what I think might work?"

Make a get-give counteroffer:

"If you (do this), *then I will* (do that)."

> Don't negotiate just to get the sale.
> Negotiate to upgrade the sale for yourself and the customer.

Chapter Sixteen

Close with the Calendar

CLOSE ON A POINT IN TIME

If a man asks, "Will you marry me," the woman says, "When?" Let's have lunch, let's meet again, let's play golf, let's make this a policy . . . These are just thoughts until a time is attached to the action. Put a date on it and you're serious. Time is the recorder of responsibility.

Time makes agreements take effect. In the long process of finding and owning a house, it becomes yours at one point in time. Your insurance coverage begins and ends at 12:01 A.M. on a certain date. Realities are pegged to points on the calendar. Even intangibles are pegged: children grow cell by cell and mature event by event until the state declares them adults. "Adult" is a concept that binds at 12:01 A.M. on a certain birthday.

DON'T TAKE *YES* FOR AN ANSWER

Many salespeople think of closing a sale as getting the customer to say *yes*. As wonderful as yes sounds, it's only a word. Too often the customer's *yes* is seen as an ending. The sale is over. Too often the *yes* becomes *yes, but* . . . , or *yes, but not now.* When *yes* is canceled by buyer's remorse, it's because *yes* is a single word without support. Without a Socratic dialogue leading to *yes*, the *yes* is not a logical conclusion the customer has reached.

DON'T BE AFRAID OF NO

Salespeople have an inordinate fear of hearing *no* from the customer. *No* thunders in their thoughts. By a word your weeks or months of effort are canceled. *No* is sliding off the raft as you go through the rapids. It's being thrown overboard from a cruise ship on a moonless night. It's striking out in the ninth inning. It's slipping out of the grasp of your trapeze partner. It's the window closing at the Motor Vehicle Bureau. It's watching your plane taxi away from the gate. *No* is the end of the world.

Many salespeople are determined that *no* will not happen and are successful at prevention. They resolutely do not ask for the business. If you don't ask, you won't be refused. Salespeople know that customers are courteous. No customer is going to say, "Look, Sue Ellen, you're not getting this business, so please leave the premises." So, the salesperson thinks, why force the issue and get myself thrown out? This customer will never get a cue to say *no*. We'll just sit here, the two of us, rehashing what has been covered or digressing to marginal points. With refusal out of the way, the salesperson feels, maybe I'll get lucky.

And do you know what? The salesperson very often does get lucky. In 80 percent of sales that close, the customer takes the initiative in closing. The customer says something like "I'd like to do this." Customer initiative isn't surprising; customers need solutions. Customers don't want to say *no!*

When the sale does close, the salesperson's reluctance to ask for the business doesn't matter. Nobody back at home base asks about it. "What went wrong?" is a question reserved for sales that don't close.

SALES MANAGERS HAVE THE SAME NIGHTMARE

The role players in a sales manager's nightmare are a customer who wants to buy and a salesperson who beats around the bush until the meeting loses its way. In the fashion of the slow-motion nightmare, follow-up meetings with the customer are scheduled, postponed, and rescheduled. At length the sales manager hears that the business that was there for the salesperson's asking has gone somewhere else.

As the nightmare continues, the rest of the manager's sales force joins the cast of characters. Now dozens of customers want to buy, and dozens of salespeople will not ask for the business. In a succession of phone calls from salespeople in the field, the manager hears that one deal after another has gone elsewhere. When the phone rings with the 10th caller on the line, the manager wakes in a sweat.

HELP THE CUSTOMER MAKE THE BUY DECISION

Closing is more enjoyable if you drop the *yes* or *no* outlook and concentrate on your job in a Socratic dialogue. Help the customer think and make decisions. The decision to buy is only more of the same. You are carrying everything forward. Use the momentum you have.

Depending on where the dialogue has traveled since you made a proposal, you may have to circle back. The customer needs to see the final agreement in the context of earlier agreements. How sharp is the customer's focus on those earlier agreements?

REGAIN MOMENTUM BY SUMMARIZING

Summarizing is necessary in two situations:

1. **Time interval.** If days or weeks have passed since your proposal, help the customer refocus on the agreements:
    - Summarize your agreement on the needs, motivators, and conditional decisions.

- Summarize your agreement on the terms of the proposal—perhaps amended by negotiation since you first made it.

2. **Intervening Questions or Objections.** If you reached an agreement on your proposal earlier in the meeting, but answering questions or negotiating objections has caused you to lose momentum, it doesn't hurt to summarize. Reviewing the points you and the customer agree on gets you back on track.

MAKE A CALENDAR STATEMENT

You are going to close on a point in time. The prior agreements are in place and are carried along in the dialogue. The customer feels their momentum. Agreeing to do business is a logical conclusion. To make doing business a serious proposition, let time give it reality. Don't wait for customer initiative. Ask for the business.

In order to do this for you, let's get out our calendars and schedule the next steps.

You and the customer have appointment books—use them. They are the useful physical markers that help you both take hold of the close. Reach down and draw your appointment book out of your briefcase.

Notice the way the calendar statement is phrased: **"In order to** do this **for you."** You are carrying out the customer's wishes! **Closing is the last of the customer's many logical conclusions in a Socratic sales dialogue.**

- You have demonstrated understanding of the customer's needs.
- You have fit a proposal to those needs—and amended it through negotiation with the customer.

- You are putting the proposal into effect. That's what closing means.

No tricks. No mystery. No fancy moves. It's a straight line. Far from dreading a *no* response, your only caution should be to avoid pressure on the customer—because at this point it's hard for the customer to say no.

SPECIFY THE NEXT STEPS

Think back to the customer's conditional decision about "when" and work from the point in time the customer gave as an answer. Your question, "If you were to go ahead . . . when would you? . . ." asked for a conditional decision. Now treat that conditional decision as a commitment. "In dreams begins responsibility."

Fred had said he'd like to begin a maintenance program for his 28 trucks in October. What's the first step to get ready for October? You may suggest a step you'd like Fred to take and identify a step you will take. You have four ways to generate next steps:

- Actions the customer offers to take.
- Actions the customer wants you to take.
- Actions you offer to take.
- Actions you want the customer to take.

"Next steps" may vary with the situation:

- If you sell from an order pad and the customer agrees to buy, then you write the order, hand the customer a copy, shake hands, and phone in the order. Those next steps take only minutes and often suffice to wrap up the business, because delivery follows.
- In other scenarios, the salesperson gets a firm commitment from the customer to do the business, but follow-through waits upon corporate counsel's drawing of the contracts. In some businesses even a qualified buyer

must submit the decision as a protocol to upper management's nod. Contracts and management approval are preliminary to many more steps.

- In many cases the next step is the first stage of implementation, which assigns a series of tasks to both salesperson and customer.
- If objections block agreement, you close on any next step that keeps the dialogue going and the deal in play. Your next step may be to return to the negotiation table with a new get-give list.

FIX THE DATES WITH EASILY ANSWERED QUESTIONS

The calendar or appointment book is composed of dates. Ask for a commitment to be written on one or more of the pages. Here's how the close might sound:

Salesperson:

Fred, in order to do this truck maintenance program for you, let's get out our calendars and schedule next steps. [Reaches for appointment book.]

Customer:

Okay. [Reaches for appointment book.]

Salesperson:

You said you'd like to be up and rolling by October. [The customer's conditional decision to begin in October is treated as a decision.] **Which date works for you?**

Customer:

Hmm. Needs to be the second week.

Salesperson:

Okay. Let's say the first truck comes in on October 12. What's the first step you need to take toward making that happen?

Customer:

I'd need to show your contract to our legal department.

Salesperson:

Fred, here's a copy of our standard contract. Now, there are steps I need you to take. By this Friday morning, I'll fax you a form for you to list model, year, and registration of all vehicles in the program. To make October 12 work for you, I'm targeting September 18. **Can you have the contract back to me by September 18?**

Customer:

Yes, I can.

Salesperson:

Also, on September 18, I'd like the list with truck model, year, and registration of all vehicles in the maintenance program? **Is that date okay for you?**

Customer:

Yes.

Salesperson:

Now, one more thing. Normally, we advise you when to bring in a truck, based on mileage. First time around, though, you have to give me dates when trucks are available. Use their registration number. **Is September 18 okay?**

Customer:

Let's make it the 21st for all these things.

Salesperson:

The 21st of September is good for me. Fred, are there any steps you want me to take other than the contract?

Customer:

If our attorneys amend the contract, I'd need it signed and over-nighted back to me because I'm out of town the next week. Probably just technicalities. I don't foresee anything big.

Salesperson:

I'll overnight it to you for arrival on the 22nd. You'll get a fax from me Friday confirming all this. We can talk on the 22nd about a briefing session for your drivers. It's great we're under way, Fred. Congratulations!

THE CUSTOMER REACHES THE LAST LOGICAL CONCLUSION

Excitement! The customer has every reason to be excited. You both have struck a deal that gives the customer a solution. It's on the way. Of course, excitement is a feeling and feelings aren't logical, but the *reason* for the customer's excitement is logical. **You and the customer have reached a final decision by drawing many conclusions.**

You supported each conclusion along the way with respect and trust. Each of you shared a perspective: the customer by painting a picture of the needs and you by a no surprises proposal. In negotiating you applied full-value listening to the interests each of you expressed. The final decision is a logical outcome.

For your part, you too have every reason to be excited.

SOCRATIC SKILLS NOTEBOOK

Help the customer make the buying decision.

   1. Regain momentum by summarizing.

   2. Make a calendar statement.

"In order to do this for you, let's get out our calendars and schedule the next steps."

   3. Specify the next steps.
- Actions the customer offers to take.
- Actions the customer wants you to take.
- Actions you offer to take.
- Actions you want the customer to take.

   4. Attach dates to all action steps.

Time is the recorder of responsibility. Close on a point in time.

Epilogue: 400 B.C., One Month Later

Darius had to wait several weeks for his first appointment with the busy Socrates. Then for two days he was instructed by Socrates, and for a week Darius pondered what he had learned. The next day at dawn he took his wagon into the hills to again visit the Olympian Construction Company. This time, he applied Socratic selling. As the sun was setting, he pulled his wagon back into the courtyard of his company's building. Crito, his manager, rushed out to meet him.

"Darius, do we have the Olympian business?"

"Socrates is right, Crito. The customer does know the truth and draws all the conclusions that lead us to it."

"How many wagon wheels did they buy?"

"Not a one, Crito."

"Not a wheel, and you ride in here smiling?"

"Wheels they can always use, but wheels are not the solution. Our solution—the conclusion I helped them reach—is a wagon maintenance program. We service all their wagons—many dozens!"

"Great wisdom of Socrates! May it be known to salespeople through the ages! It is a pity he writes nothing. There should be a book."

"Listen to more, Crito." Darius climbed down from his wagon. "Olympian Construction is doing so much business they haven't time for anything but the business they're in. They want us to 'do the worrying about the wagons,' as they put it—and as I quoted them, when I summarized their needs in my proposal."

"More, Darius. Tell me even more!"

"More indeed." They walked together across the courtyard. "Besides servicing their wagons, we will lease them our own wagons to

161

the extent their need for transport grows. We can lease them two dozen right away."

"This old Socrates can count me as a friend at his side until his last hour!"

"Beyond servicing their wagons and leasing them ours, we will train their drivers. As I helped them think about wagon maintenance, they concluded that drivers are part of the problem."

"And I conclude you're a well-taught salesperson. From this day on, dream happily of bonuses!"

"Dream happily yourself, Crito, with no more of the bad dreams of sales managers."

"Where is Socrates, that I may thank him?"

"He is gone from the Lyceum these days. But he asked me to tell you this: He will have many easily answered questions for you when he returns."

INDEX

Other books of interest to you from Irwin Professional Publishing...

NICHE SELLING
How to Find Your Customer in a Crowded Market
William T. Brooks

This dynamic tool gives you strategies for targeting customers, analyzing competitors, pricing, positioning, and capitalizing on personal selling opportunities.
ISBN: 1-55623-499-6

SOLUTION SELLING
A System for Difficult-to-Sell Products
Michael T. Bosworth

Sales professionals need a reliable method for selling products and services that are perceived as sophisticated or complex. This book offers techniques for overcoming the customer's resistance, including how to generate prospects and new business with a unique value-perception approach.
ISBN: 0-7863-0315-8

HIGH PERFORMANCE SALES ORGANIZATIONS
Best Practices From Global Sales Leaders
Kevin J. Corcoran, Laura K. Petersen, Daniel B. Baitch, and Mark TerHarr

In today's highly competitive, global marketplace, sales organizations are looking for innovative ways to differentiate themselves and gain customer loyalty. This book provides insights into the principles and practices used by some of the world's leading sales organizations. In particular, the book highlights the findings of a recent study of sales leaders in North America, Europe, and Japan.

ISBN: 0-7863-0352-2

WORLD CLASS CUSTOMER SATISFACTION

Converting Loyalty into Profits

Jonathan D. Barsky

Presents the newest customer-service techniques from around the world, in an 8-step, "how-to" program. This unique guide includes a game format that challenges and motivates readers to take the initiative and maintain increased customer satisfaction.

ISBN: 0-7863-0128-7

Available in fine bookstores and libraries everywhere.